TRAINING BIRDS OF PREY

JEMIMA PARRY-JONES

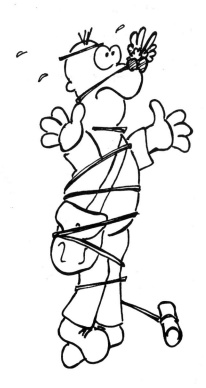

David & Charles

TO ALL BIRDS OF PREY

*Page 1   Tawny Eagle bred at the
National Birds of Prey Centre*

*Page 2   Immature Harris Hawk. Twenty years
ago this bird was hardly known in Britain, now it is
probably the most loved and popular falconry bird.
Ideal for beginners and experienced falconers alike,
its clever nature and curiosity leads it to learn and
improve with passing years. However, don't keep
Harris Hawks in seclusion aviaries or away from
visual stimulation or they will get bored. Like all
birds of prey they still need commitment to get the
best out of them*

A DAVID & CHARLES BOOK

Copyright © Jemima Parry-Jones 1994
First published 1994
Reprinted 1996, 1998
Paperback edition first published 2001

Jemima Parry-Jones has asserted her right to be identified
as author of this work in accordance with the Copyright, Designs
and Patents Act, 1988.

A catalogue record for this book is available from the British Library.

ISBN 0 7153 1238 3

Book designed by Michael Head
Typeset in Sabon by ABM Typographics Ltd, Hull
printed in Italy by LEGO SpA
for David & Charles
Brunel House   Newton Abbot   Devon

Visit our website at www.davidandcharles.co.uk

Front cover illustration: Please note that this Buzzard is wearing mews jesses specifically for the
purposes of photography. They should not be used when flying the bird.

TRAINING
BIRDS OF PREY

CONTENTS

INTRODUCTION: WHY ANOTHER FALCONRY BOOK?

Having reread the beginning of this book, I am concerned that it may seem a little negative to the reader who is hoping it will teach him or her how to train and care for a bird of prey or owl. Well, it tends to be that way, but only because I want to point out the pitfalls and help you avoid them. This book should make mistakes less likely and give you an idea of some of the philosophy behind the important elements in falconry. A good understanding of birds of prey and owl-keeping should make you enjoy it all the more and, at the same time, give any bird you might own or look after a safe, happy and comfortable life.

When I was asked to write another book on falconry I was concerned that there were more than enough already, and that I wasn't sure I could add anything useful to what has been said before. However, two reasons prompted me to go ahead. Firstly, I am still getting hundreds of phone calls per year from people who either don't know how to start in falconry, or who have started and got it all wrong. Obviously there is a need for sound, practical advice. Secondly, looking at the books that are currently available, there are some gaps, particularly on owl-keeping, that are crying out to be filled. Anyway, I needed the cash, and until I do this one, David & Charles won't let me do the one I want to do! Mind you they are being very mean, I wanted to call it *Yet Another Falconry Book* but they won't let me!

Some of the contents of this book will repeat aspects already covered in *Falconry* but I have to assume you haven't got the other book or I will leave gaps. For those who have got it I apologise; just skip them and move on!

Having been fairly circumspect in my opinions in the last book, I am damned if I am going to hold back in this one. There are some aspects of falconry emerging which are detrimental to the sport and I thought it was time someone spoke out, just to add to my already enormous popularity! Many new people coming into falconry are getting the wrong impression and ideas about falconry, the wrong advice and information, sometimes even the wrong equipment and the wrong birds. That is a very great shame because in the long term both the sport and the birds will suffer, and anyone who really knows me is aware that my primary concern is always the birds.

I am also concerned that many of those already involved with birds of prey and owl-keeping are so inept that they don't realise that their behaviour is damaging their pastime or don't even care. So be warned, this book is extremely opinionated and I make no apologies. I am going to say all those things I have been dying to say for years!

This book is aimed at those who seriously want to learn falconry. The last one I wrote was aimed at giving an understanding of falconry *before taking it up*. In fact I really wrote it, at least the falconry part, to try to put people off once they had realised what was involved. It's also good for anyone interested in captive breeding.

This book tells you:

- What sort of bird to get
- How to find out where to get one
- What sort of housing and equipment you need
- How to sort out a food supply and what to feed
- Feed supplements
- How to find a good vet

Part II covers handling, training and flying and is divided into the five groups of birds likely to be used: buzzards; owls; falcons; eagles and hawks. There is a desperate need for information on caring for owls. Basic training is pretty much the same for most of the diurnal birds, but there are important differences. There is bound to be some unavoidable repetition. Each group is tackled from the very start: collecting the bird, training, working through until flying free and ready to hunt.

I am not going into great detail on hunting with birds, as that is something that can only be learnt with time and experience. There is one *very* important thing to remember when attempting to hunt: unless you understand the countryside and the habits of whatever you are hunting you will never be very successful. Any good hunter – man or beast – understands the quarry, knows its habitat, its behaviour patterns, where it is likely to be at what time of the day, how to approach it and a million other factors as well. You must know and *respect* what you are hunting or you will never succeed. There are many good books on country lore, just look at the section in a good library. However, the best way to learn about the countryside and the creatures that live in it, is to go out quietly and, *with permission of the landowner*, observe. If you got up before dawn once a month, and just sat and watched a good country area during the day, seeing all the seasons, you would learn more than any book could teach you. If you did the same thing with someone who really knows their countryside, you would be even better informed.

Country Code and Hunting

You should learn the codes of the country, and how to behave, before flying a bird on other people's land. In the USA there are millions of acres of public land where, within the laws, you can hunt. However, in the UK all the land is owned by someone and so permission must be sought. Landowners and their fences, gates and stock must be treated with respect. If you disregard this aspect and use people and land badly you will spoil it for all of us and that is unforgivable.

Hunting with birds of prey is, like fishing, a very quiet sport and you may observe many things going on around you. Seeing a wild Tawny Owl trying furiously to conceal herself against the trunk of a holly tree, or a Sparrowhawk trying to catch a bat, hearing the first Cuckoo, or seeing a wonderful autumn sunset, are great experiences. It matters not that your bird fails to catch something that day; your understanding of our environment is greater and more enriched.

Anti-hunting people will never understand that genuine hunting people not only have a tremendous knowledge of the country, the quarry they are hunting and the habitat that it needs, but also have a realistic love for that which they are hunting.

They see its beauty, understand its mind, appreciate its ways and its fears, they see it rearing young during the breeding season. They want it to be a part of the countryside and go out of their way to ensure its long-term safety in a healthy environment. They also want to be a part of its habitat and that part includes hunting. It is because they provide a habitat and see the whole cycle of birth and life, including foxes hunting rabbits and moorhens killing ducklings, that they realise death is as natural as life. The incidental benefit to the countryside, in general, in the UK is that by providing a suitable habitat for quarry species, an enormous number of other species gain places to live and food to eat as well.

The great taboo subject with humans today is death. People don't want to think about where their meat comes from, or may even turn vegetarian because they don't like death. Many people who live in the country these days don't really understand what it is about. They like to see spring arrive but don't like mud from dogs or wellies in their houses. They like to see the new lambs but don't really think of them as potential chops in the future. They find it hard to understand why a good farmer will work to save and bottle-feed young livestock, only to send them to market when full grown. That is a part of understanding the countryside: the full cycle.

If you want a book to teach you how to catch quarry with your bird – don't buy this one! I don't believe that a book can do that anyway. If, on the other hand, you want a book that will teach you how to train your bird up to the hunting stage and a little beyond, or how to care for a bird of prey or owl, then this is the one for you!

The Future

Falconry is a very old sport, probably as old as coursing; however, I should say here that the history of falconry does not interest me in the slightest. I am far more interested in its future. Both those already involved in falconry and those who are coming into it must realise the pressure on field sports and keeping animals in captivity. Right now there is an enormous increase of interest in the welfare of animals by various groups. Falconers and bird of prey or owl-keepers should be very aware of this and make sure that their interest does actually have a future. There are many people out there just dying to stop the keeping of animals, or birds, in captivity.

The one factor which would make books such as this one unnecessary would be the licensing of individuals wanting to keep or fly birds of prey or owls. I find it very odd that in almost every other country where falconry is legal, those interested in taking up the sport have to pass a proficiency test and have a minimum standard of quarters for the birds. Yet in this nation of animal lovers, anyone can go out and buy a bird, without having any sort of licence, anywhere to keep her and no idea how to look after her.

Many reputable falconers are horrified by the attitude of pet-shop owners and, indeed, the Pet Shop Owners Association see nothing wrong in selling birds of prey to any customer in the same way that they sell budgerigars. They keep birds of prey, including some of the larger owls, in a small cage in the shop, thus implying this is an acceptable way to keep them to those uninformed members of the public who may see them. They fail to understand that it is unlikely that the budgerigars are going to go through a training period and eventually be flown free outside. They also fail to understand the temperament of a bird of prey or owl which makes her highly unsuitable to be kept in cages similar to those sold for parrots (not that parrots should be kept like that anyway). I find the attitude of some pet-shop owners extremely irresponsible and I would suggest that anyone seeing this sort of uncaring behaviour voices their disgust loudly and does not use that shop. Legally, however, there is nothing, at the moment, to stop people selling, for example, Barn Owls or Kestrels to the general public in this way. Both birds are prime examples of the worst kind of beginner's birds and the Barn Owl is a declining species in the wild. The Wildlife and Countryside Act does absolutely nothing to protect birds of prey or owls in captivity. The Cruelty to Animals Act is so out of date it is a joke and often does not give 'wildlife' any protection anyway. As the law is ineffective it is up to you and I, and others who care, to behave in a manner that will hopefully make people realise that birds of prey should not be sold in this way.

For those who are considering keeping a bird of prey, be aware of the responsibility you are taking on in caring not only for a bird, be it an owl, a falcon or even an eagle, but also for the reputation of an ancient, respected, and in terms of conservation, valuable sport. If you have a bird of prey, whether you like it or not, the general public will think you are a falconer.

Developing an Interest

One of the more common questions asked of me is 'How did you get interested in falconry?' and actually, I am quite the wrong person to answer that one. I was born into it, I am a third generation falconer so, for me, falconry has always been there and will, I hope, continue that way. But it does make me wonder how other people come to falconry. Consequently, I realise that this is one of my major worries/dislikes, and to make things worse I am, in part, responsible for it. So the question is: 'How did *you* get interested?' There is a reason behind asking this question. These days, not all you see to do with falconry is necessarily the way it *should* be done.

Some people get interested after reading books, although I think that this is probably not the most normal way. If it was and you read T. H. White's *The Goshawk*, please don't think that is the way to train a bird of prey: it's rubbish, a good literary book, but a rubbish way of training birds. Most people will have either seen something on TV, seen a falconry demonstration at a village fête, or agricultural show or perhaps seen someone at a show with an owl. Some will have been to centres like mine and have gained an interest from that.

Falconry Centres

When we first started The National Birds of Prey Centre it was called The Falconry Centre. It was the only one of its kind in the UK for at least twelve years. Now the name 'Falconry Centre' has become a generic term and there are 'falconry centres' mushrooming up all over the place. You find them in the grounds of stately homes, in garden centres, as part of other tourist attractions, in fact almost anywhere. Some are OK, a very few are good, an awful lot are very poor, and sadly the Zoo Act, which should be controlling any new collection of wildlife opening to the public, is administered by the wrong people, and is therefore ineffective.

The problem with the less good centres is twofold. Either the people running them have very little experience and so are often handing on the wrong information to the visiting public, *or* they are employing young (cheap) labour who are very keen on falconry but just don't have the training or knowledge to be able to keep the birds well, or hand out expertise to visitors. I don't have anything against youth, but it takes many years of experience to be able to get to the stage where you can safely hand on knowledge, and even longer to gain the courage and understanding to admit that you don't know everything there is to know. My main concern is how are the public to know if they are being given good or bad information? Many of these places keep their birds badly, set a poor example and give totally the wrong impression to potential beginners as to how they should house and care for a bird.

Courses

The same principles apply to falconry courses. As the economic situation worsens and unemployment increases, some of those interested in falconry are taking to teaching falconry as a good method of making or supplementing a living. To learn falconry properly, in my opinion, you must go on a minimum of a five-day course (consecutive days). At least you get some continuity with a bird, can see how the weight drops and what to look for in the way of problems. *You must always remember that if you make a mistake in handling or training a bird you can kill it.* I know of one person who, as a complete novice, went on a course run by friends of mine and within a few months had got together his own birds and was running courses himself! However, don't despair, there are good courses to be found, you just have to do a little homework first and use your commonsense to find them.

Falconry Furniture

Watch out for a similar situation developing in the falconry furniture world. There is some very poorly made equipment about at the moment. If you find that the people you are getting your equipment from suggest that you don't need a hood for a Kestrel, don't hang up on them: it may not be the advice you want, but it's sound advice. Have a look at the equipment at centres that you feel are good quality and ask them where they get it from. Again, use your commonsense and patronise those people who have the well-being of the birds at heart.

Shows and Demonstrations

I have been giving falconry demonstrations at agricultural shows, game fairs, village fêtes and the like for the last twenty-six years. I was pretty much the only person doing them for quite a while. So, in fact, I have probably been guilty, by example, of encouraging others to do the same and possibly to take up falconry. I have justified that over the years by thinking that I have done far more good by improving people's understanding and admiration of birds of prey than I have done harm by encouraging the wrong people to take up the sport. I did hope that by doing the best possible demonstrations I could, and having the best-built centre I could manage, those who took up the sport would try and keep their standards high: *I was wrong*.

At present, there must be close to a hundred different people/groups giving demonstrations, a *very few* are good and have thought about what they are doing. Others quite obviously are idiots, know very little about falconry, have very poor quality demonstration birds and, worse, are putting over the subject quite wrongly to the general public. Often these people are very good at getting money out of companies for sponsorship. So you can decide for yourself, the following paragraphs set out what I consider to be either irresponsible, poorly thought out, or downright stupid behaviour.

Shelter

Birds should not be on view to the public with no shelter from either the weather, people or dogs. If anyone is putting on a static display of birds of prey they should make sure that the show puts up suitable quarters for the birds, just as they do when they have cattle, cats, dogs and the like on display. I feel very strongly about this: it is the responsibility of the show committee to ensure that those birds are housed safely, it is impossible for the demonstrator to put up suitable quarters in the time he or she will be on site. The responsibility of the falconer is to refuse to display the birds unless the quarters are up to standard.

Some demonstrators leave tethered birds unattended which is insane. Leaving birds in strong sun in hot weather with no protection can and does kill them.

Tethered Owls

Owls should not be tethered and they look awful at shows. They are much happier living in a nice aviary at home and, if they have to be travelled, they love a nice *large* dark box.

Injured Wild Birds

Displaying injured wild birds at shows, often to raise money, is unforgivable. Unless you have a special licence from the Department of the Environment it is *illegal*.

Mixing Tethered and Flying Birds

It is totally wrong to fly birds in an arena with other birds sitting tethered on field cages or perches in the flying area. The tethered birds may be grabbed and injured or even killed by the loose bird that is flying. Even if there is someone attending the tethered birds they are unlikely to be fast enough to stop a bird being grabbed.

Public Participation

Untrained adults and children should not fly birds at shows: this is irresponsible. A child may suddenly get frightened and drop his/her fist at the last moment, the bird might hit the child by accident because its perch has just been removed and it can't stop in time. Such behaviour might make that child frightened of birds for the rest of his/her life. Someone once said to me that using the birds to fly to children and adults was an educational tool introducing them to falconry and birds of prey. Well I *totally disagree*. This gives the wrong impression, falconry is a complicated sport with the life of a bird at stake. By all means teach people, privately, where you are in control of the situation, but not in front of a huge audience, making the whole thing look like a circus act and encouraging people to think that flying birds of prey is easy. We have been teaching people here since we opened in 1967 and we have never had to resort to this sort of thing. There are far better ways to educate people.

Poor Travelling Conditions

If exhibitors are not prepared to set up a vehicle that is designed for maximum comfort for their livestock they should not be accepting demonstration work. They are, usually, being paid to go, therefore some of the money should be invested for the comfort of the birds. Our vans have built-in boxes where the birds have room to sit on perches, hop off, turn around or whatever. If we are using our smaller van, we don't travel more than four birds and preferably three.

The BFSS recommendations are that no more than six birds should be on display, as this is the number that can be travelled safely in a medium-sized van and can be cared for by one person without too many problems. If you see ten or more birds all tethered very close together then you are looking at birds owned by one, or several, idiots. I have seen this behaviour at shows over the last three years and it saddens me to think that there are people who think so little of their birds or their sport.

I list all these abhorrent practices because you, as a beginner, may have become interested because of a demonstration, or you may go to see one to obtain advice. Please consider this: if you see someone doing *any* of the foregoing, they are not the people either to get advice from or to be taught by because they don't have either the birds' welfare or the sport's well-being at heart.

Many falconers will say I have opened a can of worms and these problems should not be aired in public. However, most of these observations have been pointed out to me by members of the public in the first place. It is imperative that we get our house in order. It doesn't mean there are no good falconers, bird of prey or owl centres, rehabilitators or keepers of birds of prey and owls, there are hundreds of them! There are also bad ones and these should be routed out, exposed and perhaps educated to do better.

Falconry and the keeping of birds of prey and owls has achieved many wonderful things over the years:

- Enormous strides have been made in curing disease and injuries in both captive and wild birds of prey and owls, and we are still learning.
- We understand the nutritional requirements of birds of prey and owls to a far greater extent.
- We can now breed many endangered species to replenish wild stocks.
- We can also release birds into the wild and ensure their survival.
- Handling and training a bird of prey, or owl, gives a greater insight into the species' needs and desires. Much more is learnt than by simple observation.

So, as with anything, there are the good sides and bad. The bad should be exposed and changed and the good should be recognised and encouraged in order that we might continue to learn and improve wherever possible.

New Controls

At the time of writing there are now codes of conduct being worked upon by experienced and caring people to cover the various disciplines in falconry and bird of prey and owl-keeping.

The Hawk and Owl Trust, together with The Hawk Board, is producing a code of conduct for those involved in rehabilitation; The Federation of Zoos is working on a code of conduct for zoos using birds of prey and owls in demonstrations; the British Field Sports Society, with the aid of The Hawk Board, is drawing up a code of conduct for those giving falconry demonstrations and also for the show organisers; The British Field Sports Society Parliamentary Subcommittee for Falconry and The Hawk Board are doing a code of welfare and husbandry for birds of prey. This will apply to *all* people keeping birds of prey and owls for breeding, falconry or just as pets.

Those people who are experienced and care for their birds and their sport are putting in a great deal of time and effort to make sure that their house is in order.

How Do I Start?

Although books and videos are a great source of information and a very valuable tool to have around, they are not enough to teach you how to train a bird and particularly will not help you when things start to go wrong and you need 'hands on' advice. Nor do they give you 'hands on' experience.

Without doubt the best way to start is to go on a course. Now the question is how do you know a good course from a bad one? This can be a problem because, as a beginner, how the hell do you know which is which! The same problem is going to occur when trying to learn anything new. I used to be able to recommend courses with no feelings of guilt because we stopped giving them in 1985 and I had no axe to grind. In 1992 we started courses again partly because of the recession (and a financial need) and partly because there were so many requests. So now I have an axe to grind, it makes it harder to say who is good and who is bad.

Falconry Centres
If you have an interest in falconry or bird of prey and owl-keeping then you should visit some of the centres around the country. It's no good saying: 'There are none in my area so I can't go for advice or help', that is a *pathetic* attitude and if you can't be bothered to make the effort then you shouldn't be thinking of keeping any living creature. It is a different matter if you can't afford to travel to centres, but quite frankly if you can't, and I hate to be hard on you, you should not be considering taking up falconry or keeping a bird of prey. It is an expensive sport and if you are short of funds how are you going to afford to build decent quarters, or pay vets' bills if the bird needs help? If there is no local falconry centre, bird of prey or owl centre you will just have to travel to where they are located. By going to *several* of these places you should be able to differentiate between those that are good and those that are not. Look at the aviaries: are they clean and well built with good perches, or are they built of fence panels or old timber off-cuts and look tatty and untidy? Do the

birds look well? Are the staff of a reasonable age to be experienced and do they sound confident? Are all the birds well sheltered from the cold, wet and extreme heat, are they secure from interference from the visitors or do they appear to have nowhere to go if it rains? Can people get right up to them? Does the place give an impression of health and tidiness, or does it look run down as if people don't really care? Do try to go to several centres as you will be able to make comparisons, otherwise how can you tell? When you have found a good one, go on their course, or follow their advice.

Clubs

Try to join a bird of prey breeders or falconry club. You will meet other people with the same interests as yourself. The British Field Sports Society has addresses of some of the clubs. In fact you should be a member of the BFSS as it is the only useful pressure group which keeps an eye on Parliament and the EC. They monitor new legislation and fight it if necessary.

You should, by now, begin to have an idea of who knows their stuff. Then, and only then, ask for advice. Use your brains and commonsense. There are, unfortunately, lots of people who just love to give advice, but sadly many of them should not be doing so. Often if you *think* about what people tell you, you can see if it is good value or not.

Courses

Ask the people running the centres where you might go for courses. Many of them will have various leaflets advertising courses. If they are worth their salt, they will have leaflets from more than one establishment, so that they can be seen to be being open-minded. Some may even run courses themselves but, remember, if the place looks seedy and the birds don't look great, the quality of the course may well be similar. Ask other members of the club that you join. You may well get conflicting advice, but by asking questions you should be able to sort out the good from the bad. You can also talk to the people who are giving courses and question them a little on the phone as to what they teach, what sort of birds you will be using and so on. If they are using or advising Barn Owls or Kestrels kick them into touch immediately. Neither of these species should be used for beginners in falconry, even on courses.

Once you have sorted out your course, forget about birds until you have been on it. It is very hard to do but there is nothing more infuriating than teaching people who have either read a lot of books or taken a lot of advice and then start trolling it out on the course in front of others. Not only will you alienate yourself from the people teaching the course, but you will find that any other members on the course will eventually get very bored with you. If you have prior knowledge keep it to yourself and limit yourself to asking questions, within reason. One of the hardest things to do is to keep quiet but, in the long run, you will learn more and enjoy yourself more by doing so, you will also be more popular. No one likes a smart arse!

Occasionally we have had people on a course who have already built the quarters for the bird, bought the equipment and so on. Sadly they have often wasted not only their time, but also their money. Go on the course first, learn what bird you should get for your circumstances, what sort of quarters it will need, how to care for, feed and manage it, how to train it if it happens to be a bird you want to fly and then go home and get everything ready for the prospective new bird. Very often we find that once people do go on a course they will decide that, in fact, they just don't have enough time to dedicate to a bird and will perhaps consider getting a bird when their circumstances have changed. Some people find that the course makes them realise that falconry or birds of prey are just not for them – this is great – hopefully they will have had a wonderful time, learnt a good deal but had the sense and honesty to admit they don't want the commitment of a bird. Some finish the course and decide that they do want to continue and get a bird and feel that with the experience they have gained on the course, they can manage.

You might be one of those lucky people who knows someone involved in falconry or the keeping of birds of prey or owls and who is willing to teach you the basics. But, do beware, some people, however well meaning, may not be keeping their birds as well as they might, or may not be as knowledgeable as they think they are. It is a difficult situation, but again, by visiting the centres, you will have picked up a little knowledge and should be able to judge whether or not you consider the person suitable to teach you. You may also find that by joining one of the clubs you can start in an apprenticeship scheme. In this way you will go out with other falconers or bird of prey keepers and learn, through them, how to look after a bird correctly. This is a much more drawn-out way of learning as you are only able to have assistance and training when the people teaching have spare time. But it will give you a good basic knowledge and hopefully you will make friends with people of like minds.

You are probably wondering why I am even bothering to write this book. A five-day course is great but, by the time you have sorted out the requirements for a bird and organised obtaining one, you will have forgotten some of what you learnt. This book will remind and guide you through those early, important, difficult and scary first weeks. Use it as a teaching aid that can be referred to at any time.

PART I

HOW TO START

CHAPTER ONE

WHAT BIRD SHOULD I GET?

To a great extent this question will be answered in Part II, but it will also depend on what you want to do. If you just want a bird as a pet, ie not to hunt, to live in a nice roomy aviary in your garden and perhaps be trained and flown free, then you need to go for one of the species that are naturally lazy and will do almost anything rather than go out and hunt.

A word of warning here for those who keep other types of birds. If you have aviaries in your garden with finches, softbills, parrot-like birds, or even pheasants, they will all be extremely upset if you start to keep any birds of prey, particularly owls, where they can see them. They treat birds of prey as enemies and it is unfair to try to mix the two. Breeding birds will probably stop breeding and you may well find that the stress of having birds of prey or owls close by causes infection and death. If you must mix the types, make sure that your birds of prey and owls are well out of sight from other species of birds. The same goes for prey species of mammals. It is unkind to keep rabbits next to Goshawks, for example!

Beginner's Birds

Small birds are not good beginner's birds so Kestrels, Barn Owls, Tawny Owls, Little Owls, Merlins and Sparrowhawks, and many others of that size, should not be considered by anyone wanting to train a bird of prey to fly free. Why? Very simple: the smaller the bird, the easier it is to kill with inexperience. All of these birds weigh under 1lb (0.5kg) and in some cases a good deal less. If the weight is brought down too low during the training period then the bird may well die. A weight as small as $\frac{1}{2}$oz (15g) can mean a matter of life or death to the smaller species. Wait until you are more experienced before you take on *any* of the smaller species, by then not only will you have learnt how to deal with the incredibly variable weights of birds of prey and owls, but you may not want to bother with many of the smaller birds. Don't get me wrong, I don't have anything against the smaller species, indeed I care about them enough to want them left alone by beginners. Birds are not easier to train because they are larger, but the mistakes you make do them less harm. Being larger they can absorb a weight loss with less detriment to their health and they are less easy to kill.

Many people are going to be upset by these statements and say that they started with a Barn Owl or bought one for their child and everything went fine – but what you people do not know is how many Barn Owls get killed by people just like you when everything *didn't* go fine. You don't get the phone calls from the people with sick birds with no idea how to treat them, you don't see the young birds after they have been given the wrong diet with their legs and wings twisted wrecks. So you

Bilberry, a 1½-year-old Harris Hawk

don't have to feel the fury and anger that we, who do see both sides of the story, feel, and are impotent to do anything about.

If you bought this book because you wanted help and advice and care about the birds, then listen to what is sound advice gained from a lifetime's experience of seeing the good and the bad sides of keeping and training birds of prey and owls. If you are going to ignore the advice then not only have you just wasted your money, but you will probably end up making a mistake that will result in the death of the bird and personally I have no time for, or patience with, that sort of person.

Suitable Species

For those wanting to keep and fly diurnal (active in daylight) birds of prey, the best ones to start with are Harris Hawks, Common Buzzards and Red-tailed Buzzards. If you absolutely have to start with a falcon, then a Lanner Falcon is probably the best, but you would do much better to have a couple of years with a broadwing first. For those interested in flying owls, I don't think you can better a Bengal Eagle Owl, they are medium sized, generally have a nice temperament and are easily manageable. I will go into far more detail on the individual species in Part II. I shall be covering a little on the true hawks – the *accipiters* and the eagles – but neither of these should be considered as beginner's birds under any circumstances.

Finding a Suitable Bird

Note: For the sake of ease I will refer to all birds as female from now on. This has no significance other than convenience; all the information is relevant to both sexes.

There are now many people breeding birds of prey and owls. Some are breeding them purely because they want to have the availability of a home-bred bird whenever they need one but, at the same time, they may have a surplus which they sell on to cover the costs of captive breeding. (And believe me when I say it is costly!) Some breed purely to sell to others and some of these breeders are excellent and put in a lot of effort to produce good quality birds. Others don't appear to give a damn what they produce or how they do it: these people are to be avoided.

Dealers

Avoid those who don't breed their own birds but, instead, buy in from others in bulk numbers and then sell the birds on. These are probably the worst people of all to obtain a bird from because, most of the time, you have no come-back if there is a problem: you will probably not know who bred the bird originally and you will not know her history. Don't go to this sort of dealer, and this includes pet shops and garden centres who now appear to be going in for selling birds of prey and, more particularly, owls. I very strongly disapprove of raptors and owls being sold in such places and I don't give a damn who knows it! If we all cut out the dealers and middle men then eventually they will cease to exist as sellers of birds of prey and owls, and this will be a great achievement.

Importers

Be wary of the supply of birds from abroad. Some people are importing large numbers of captive-bred birds from Canada and the USA. Many of these are excellent birds, but some are not. There are breeders abroad who are just producing large numbers for sale regardless of quality. If a bird has been imported you will have even less chance of returning her should problems arise. So just because a bird is imported it does not necessarily mean it is OK or better than British-produced birds, so be careful.

Reputable Breeders

If you have taken my advice and visited a few centres, joined a club, possibly gone on a course and are generally far more knowledgeable than you were when you first got interested, you will be able to find people who can advise you on a good source of birds. If you do get the name and address of a good breeder, it is probably advisable to reserve a bird as the good breeders often have a waiting list for their birds, particularly some of the less common owls bred in the UK.

The British Falconers Club produces a magazine for their members in which breeders of birds advertise. There is a magazine called *The Falconer*, which is improving greatly now, where birds are advertised; this is available by subscription (see Useful Addresses). Probably the biggest marketplace for advertisements is a paper called *Cage and Aviary Birds* which can be ordered from any newsagents.

When you phone up about a bird that is advertised ask the following questions to find out if the person owning the bird knows much about her:

- How old is the bird?
- What sex is it?
- Is she healthy and in good feather condition?
- How was she reared?
- How is she being kept at the moment – tethered or loose in a pen?
- If tethered, when was she last flown?
- Has she been trained?
- Why is she for sale?
- What price?
- Is there any sort of guarantee?

Birds to Avoid

Personally I don't like having birds that have been trained by others, although it occasionally happens. If a bird has been tethered for a long period without being flown, she may be unfit and possibly difficult to get fit. If she is a young bird, ie four to six months old and isn't in good feather order then there may be a problem. If she is older, she may be due for, or in, a moult, in which case she may look a little tatty. I suppose the question that interests me the most is, why is the bird available? Avoid birds that have had several owners. It is very sad but, if a bird has gone from person to person, she usually is a problem. If she wasn't at the beginning she probably will be after several owners! Asking how a bird is reared is very important if you want to avoid imprinted birds.

Imprinted Birds

There are many different sorts of imprinting and there is a great deal we do not yet know about it. However, there are several forms of imprinting that do affect the behaviour of a captive bird of prey, some adversely. For example, a bird can be imprinted on one type of food. This usually happens because the breeder only feeds one food type, the commonest sort being day-old cockerels. This is a damn nuisance and can be detrimental to the bird. Firstly, any breeder who does not give his birds a variety of food items is not doing a good job, in my opinion. Secondly, trying to train a bird that has only been fed chicks either means you have to continue using chicks, which are very bad for training birds and disgusting to feed on the fist, or you have to try and change the food type prior to, or during, training. This puts added stress on a new bird and that is never a good thing.

An imprinted bird in the context of being a problem to train for flying is a bird that has been hand-reared. She hasn't seen parents or foster parents and so considers humans to be her parents. Once you get to the stage of cutting down weight she will behave very badly. She will scream for food and attention at all times, sometimes even at night. She will mantle on the fist and on food, she may be extremely aggressive and fly at the trainer.

I believe that some books suggest that an imprinted Common Buzzard will be better at hunting than a nice sound parent-reared one, because she will be more aggressive. True, but she will also be more aggressive with you, will mantle on the fist, be difficult to get off the lure, dummy rabbit or a kill, will scream, often incessantly, and generally be a pain in the arse. I wouldn't accept an imprinted buzzard as a gift!

Some people may want an imprinted bird to use as a specialised breeding bird, but that is not the subject of this book and so will not be covered. Generally an imprinted bird, apart from the owls and other exceptions mentioned above, is not a pleasant bird to have and the larger buteos and eagles can be potentially dangerous if handled badly. What any sensible beginner should want in a diurnal bird of prey is a nicely mannered, quiet, mentally well-balanced bird that will train well, be nice to live with, hunt well and possibly have the chance, at a later date, of breeding naturally with her own kind.

Hand/Cresh/Parent Rearing

Birds, other than owls (I will ignore vultures and Secretary Birds as it is unlikely that, as a beginner, you will have either of these groups of birds), are often far easier to handle when they have been hand-reared *until* you get to training them and cutting their weight down. Then the problems begin. That is one of the reasons why, if possible, you should get a guarantee with your new bird so that should it show badly imprinted behaviour you can return it to the breeder.

It is 'over' hand-rearing and cresh-rearing that tends to cause the problem. Many of our birds are hand-reared for the first few days, but once they are ringed, which is usually at ten days old, they are returned to parent- or foster-parent birds. These days our new pens are so easy to manage that we often get young back at three or four days old. If they are hand-reared too long, or hand-reared completely, they will have imprint tendencies. 'Cresh-reared' just means that the breeder has hand-reared the birds until they are picking up food for themselves and then left them in groups to be reared together. They are left with fresh food and given little or no attention by humans but as they have no parent there to feed them, there is no bonding and usually when they are trained, as full grown birds, they will revert to imprint behaviour.

A bird that has been hand-reared or cresh-reared will probably mantle badly on the fist, the perch or the ground when she has food. Mantle means to open her wings and try to hide the food with them. A badly mantling bird will drop her head, hide the food with her wings and some are impossible to pick up with food as they will keep turning round, ruining their tail in the process and will almost lie down on the food. She will, most likely, scream whenever she sees or hears you, or possibly any humans. I have heard of people quite desperate with screaming birds that are even doing it at 3am in the morning and the neighbours beginning to get pretty upset about it. (Harris Hawks can start to scream even when parent-reared, see Chapter 9.) She may be very footy, ie constantly trying to grab your bare hand with her foot. Some will even have a go at the trainer while flying. All of this is very unpleasant and can be easily avoided by making sure that you only obtain a bird that has been parent-reared.

Oddly enough this sort of behaviour does not happen in the same way with the owls, probably because they are not related to other birds of prey and so have different behaviour. I think it also has something to do with their eyesight. Nor is there the same behaviour between siblings (brothers and sisters).

I can't stress enough how much nicer a well-balanced, parent-reared diurnal bird of prey is for the owner, and all concerned, than an imprinted bird that is mentally unbalanced, and a misery to herself and the rest of humanity. Imprinted birds are also unlikely to be much use for breeding unless you are very lucky.

Price/Deposit

When you have managed to locate a recommended breeder and have ordered a bird, first make sure you confirm the price. Many breeders will ask for a deposit so you should have the price in writing anyway. Check that the breeder will keep you informed of progress, ie if all his birds fail to lay, he will know by June that he is unlikely to be able to let you have a bird and should return your deposit. This should give you enough time to find another source. He or she may even suggest another breeder at this stage. Most importantly, ask how he rears the young he produces. Apart from owls and some of the odder species like small vultures and Secretary Birds, you want to avoid hand-reared, and therefore imprinted, birds.

At The National Birds of Prey Centre we ask everyone who orders a bird from us to write in giving their experience, what bird they want, why, and to send a photo of the quarters they have for the bird. Wherever possible we like to check that potential new owners do know what they are doing or have been on a reputable course. We also like to see where our birds are going to live, hence the need for the photograph. Occasionally we write back advising that the quarters are too small. Be warned, all bar two other bird of prey centres that I or members of my staff have seen, have their weathering mews or 'hawk walk' too small for the birds, so don't take them as an example. I think there must be someone recommending 6x6ft (1.8x1.8m) quarters for Harrises and all buzzards, and I am afraid I will have to disagree here. This size is OK for falcons and small hawks but that is about all. Every other bird tethered here at the centre has a compartment 10ft (3m) wide and at least 6ft (1.8m) deep.

For those looking for owls I will go into detail as to the best sort to get for beginners, what sort of rearing methods will give you the best bird and the best age to get one, when I come on to Chapter 6.

Guarantee

If you want to avoid problems ask for a guarantee. Badly reared birds or ones with problems that are not visible immediately should be returned to the breeder/seller as early as possible, who should refund the cost of the bird. You must, of course, return the bird in the same condition you received her in. If you have a guarantee that lasts, say, for a week then at least you can have the bird checked over by your vet, have a blood sample and mute sample taken and then be confident that the bird is healthy. If you can get a guarantee against the bird being imprinted – better still. We give one here and occasionally take back a bird if there are problems, although I have to say that usually the problems are caused by the new owners and we soon cure them.

Timing

The best time to get a bird is late summer but this is tricky with owls (see Chapter 6). By late summer, August/September, most birds are full grown, hard down (feathers all out of the blood and hardened off) and should have become independent of their parents. If possible, it is a good idea for breeders to remove young from the parents' aviary once they are full grown and let them mature a little in a group without any adult birds around them. This is not always possible as space is usually at a premium. We are lucky here at The National Birds of Prey Centre. We have just recently rebuilt some pens giving us an indoor Hawk Walk to winter the trained, tethered birds and four very nice Moulting Pens for winter moulting, which double as Baby Pens in the summer. So most of our young, particularly the Harris Hawks, will have been placed in one of these after fledging and be independent of their parents before leaving us.

Late summer is good for the young birds as they are ready to begin training, and flying, without being too wild and yet should have had time to forget their parents and become adult. Another reason later summer is good is – the weather! It is a wonderful time to train young birds. Long, light evenings for plenty of manning, and warm days so that reducing weight is less traumatic. Mild weather takes the worry out of cutting down the weight of a young bird. Training birds in the winter when the temperatures can be very low is nerve racking and to be avoided by the beginner. Try to organise your holiday to coincide with the period of the new bird's training.

You should, by now, have enough knowledge to find a good source for a bird. Take your time, use your commonsense, ask for advice, do some research and don't buy the first thing that is offered to you.

CHAPTER TWO

QUARTERS FOR BIRDS OF PREY AND OWLS

I will go into more detail on quarters for birds in Part II. However, the principles behind the structure are much the same be your new bird a falcon, hawk, buzzard, owl or eagle. The only difference is size.

Aviary

Most birds do better kept loose in a good aviary once they are trained. Even such nervous birds as Black Sparrowhawks do well in specialised pens. It is, without doubt, the *only* way to keep any owl.

Aviaries remove the worry of tethered birds getting tangled when unattended, remove the stigma of having birds tethered over an extended period, keep a bird fitter, make them more secure from vandals, thieves and predators such as foxes, dogs, cats, etc. The effect of cold weather is far less with loose birds and the birds are generally happier if kept loose once they are tame. However, in the early stages, except for a hand-reared owl, your bird will have to be tethered until she is tame enough to come happily to the fist whenever you arrive on the scene. She may also need tethering after each moult, just for a few days to remind her of the training and what is expected. So design your aviary accordingly.

Over the years we have built many quarters for birds here at the Centre, we have also kept most species, both loose and tethered, that are likely to be used in the UK today. I am now pretty pleased with the way most of the Centre is looking and the way the birds are housed.

Weather Conditions

Whenever designing housing for livestock your first consideration should be the year-round weather conditions. These will pretty much dictate what you need to provide for a bird to give her a comfortable and long life. You will have to avoid the bird getting overheated in hot summer weather, too wet during those wonderful prolonged periods of heavy rain we seem to be getting these days and too cold during periods of frosty winter weather.

Some people think that an aviary that is half covered is the best, giving the bird the chance to get wet and cold or keep dry depending on where she sits. I am not impressed with the brains of most of my birds during inclement weather! They seem to be very perverse and sit looking miserably cold and wet in our older pens, even though there is plenty of shelter. We have worked with totally covered pens for six years now and I would not build anything else. Their only disadvantage is that the rain does not do some of the washing of the pen for you. But as we like to catch up the birds once a year to check them over, worm them, give the aviaries a winter clean and, in the breeding pens, build new nests ready for the breeding season, it really doesn't matter that they don't get washed by rain. The advantages far outweigh the disadvantages.

A completely roofed pen is a stronger structure and so is better for the high winds that have become a part of our weather over the last six years, they also stop the problem of snow bringing down wire or netting roofs. This is only if you build a decent structure in the first place, I hasten to add. The bird can get wet if she wants to because it is rare that rain falls totally vertically, so some is bound to get driven into the aviary; a very few of our birds will go out of their way to get wet on rainy days. However, the majority sit comfortably out of the wind and rain.

If you build a roof with plenty of light panels there will be more than enough sunlight, at the same time there are some very good materials that will insulate the bird from excessive heat. We have been underestimating the problem of low temperatures with our birds, in the UK, for a long time.

The cold we have in the British Isles is very different from that in, say, Canada or the USA for example. That is a dry cold and much more tolerable for man and beast. Ours tends to be a damp cold that is difficult to combat. Wing-tip oedema is a problem that aviary and tethered birds can get (although it is much rarer in aviary birds but quite common in tethered birds). Birds of prey have fairly poor circulation to their feet and wings, ie their extremities. Low temperatures can damage that circulation, causing the wing to develop cold, wet blisters on the lower joint. Usually, by the time you see symptoms, such as the bird either holding one or both wings away from her body or dropping them slightly, it is too late, and permanent damage is done unless you are very lucky and work very hard on the bird. You need to get to a decent vet and he or she will tell you what to do. By 'too late' I mean that the chances are the wing tips, along with part of the bones, may well shrivel and die over a few months and eventually part of the wing will fall off. At best you may find that the feathers drop out and when they regrow they are twisted. However, it is much better to avoid wing-tip oedema altogether.

In 1981, when we had a very very cold spell of freezing weather, we had one bird at the Centre, who always roosted on the ground when tethered, go down with frost bite on her toes. To this very day her toes, those she has left, will crack and split in cold weather if she is kept outside. She spends the winter inside.

Heating

We have just fitted small, low voltage, tubular heaters underneath the new perches in our new indoor Hawk Walk. As I write, the weather forecast is for Arctic weather coming down in three days with very low temperatures and we will be able to sit inside knowing that all our valuable trained, tethered birds that we love dearly are snug and warm. When you have fourteen to twenty-eight birds being flown per day it is almost impossible to have each bird loose in an individual pen. I wish we could as it would save a great deal of time. Instead we get over the problem of cold by having a purpose-built indoor Hawk Walk housing sixteen birds, which is the maximum number we fly through the winter anyway.

One of the new perches in our indoor Hawk Walk, where all the trained birds winter. Note the heater

Finding a Good Site

Check with your local council with regard to planning regulations, and apply for permission *before* you start construction.

Build your aviary facing away from the cold winds, making sure that if it is facing a prevailing, but less cold wind, there is a part of the pen that is sheltered at all times. South-facing is usually the best as it will get nice winter sun and the southerly winds are usually the kindest. Avoid putting aviaries under trees, they restrict the light, tend to be damp and there is always the risk of branches being blown onto the aviary. Autumn leaves also block gutters easily.

Make sure that it is not sited near compost heaps or muck heaps. Both of these can harbour *Aspergillus* spores. A friend of mine had his Goshawk in a weathering pen next to a compost heap and the heap was turned to get the good stuff to the top and cover the fresh stuff, the Goshawk was dead in a week: aspergillosis.

Drainage

The first thing to do once you have decided where to build your quarters is to put down some drainage. Even if you are not going to roof the pen totally you will need to get roof water away. Damp pens are very bad for birds, we have enough bloody dampness in this country without adding to it! Either dig a deep soakaway or put in a trench with a flexi-drain and take the water away, downhill, and fill a nice pond, or something useful.

Foundations

We then put down a hardcore base larger than the building that we are going to put up so we have an edge all around the building where nothing grows. Once the base is down you can work on the site in all weathers without ending up ploughing around in mud up to your privates and hating every minute of it! Believe me, I have done it and it's no fun. The last building we did it rained 4in (10cm) in one day while we were digging the foundations, none of us had a stitch of clothing on that was dry and there was not a smile to be seen (which is very rare in this place). During that building stint we had a month of rain, two weeks of freezing fog and two weeks of gales, then, just as we finished a building that should have taken three weeks instead of eight, the weather changed and was lovely. Avoid building in the winter if you can!

Design

All our aviaries have a service passage which is dark. This gives you security in several ways. Firstly, you automatically have a double-door system to prevent a bird from escaping. Secondly, if the passage is dark it will be much easier to get your bird through the doors without her getting upset. Thirdly, it is better for security from those who might want to steal your bird, in addition to being easier to look after the pen as well. Fourthly, it means you are not approaching a keen bird with wire between you and her. By coming in through a dark passage, the bird may be very excited but should not be flying into wire trying to get to you. We build our passage at least 4ft (1.2m) wide, and preferably 5ft (1.5m) as it allows the passage of a wheelbarrow without damaging your hands.

Construction

All our newer pens are built with tanalised timber. We build them in one of two ways:

1   We sink stanchions into the ground, set in concrete, and these form the structure to build on. Then we build a low brick or block wall all around the aviary between the stanchions on a shallow foundation. This keeps the bulk of the timber and all the cladding away from the ground and so it will last longer.
2   Or we may build the wall on a good foundation, with no stanchions, and then fix panels onto the wall. This is a more difficult way of building. We have only done it with one block and in some ways I wish we had done it the other way. This way the roof is built onto the panels and is not so strong. With stanchions in the ground you end up with a framework that is much easier to fill in.

Once the stanchions are in, the roof timbers go up and the whole thing becomes a strong structure should you get a sudden spell of wind. Next we build the low brick wall between the outside stanchions. We then put down a concrete floor to the service passage. This means it will never get muddy, you can sweep it easily, push a full barrow down without getting stuck, and make the whole thing much nicer to work with. We do not lay the floor in the pen itself until almost the last thing, as we can then check that all nails and bits and pieces are picked up before the sand goes down.

The next job is to clad the sides down to about 4in (10cm) below the brickwork. You can do the brickwork last, after the cladding, but it is much easier to get it done before, and then clad. With our barns, the cladding is 6x¾in (150x19mm) tanalised end boarding, nailed with galvanised nails onto 6x2½in (150x63mm) rails. The sizes of timber I am giving are suitable for our barns, but if you are building a smaller structure, then choose your timber sizes accordingly. If, however, you want a word of good advice: always overbuild rather than underbuild, that way you won't come out one day and find your aviary and birds blown away. With the Small Falcon Block we used 6x¾in (150x19mm) tanalised feather edge which we overlapped with a 2in (50mm) overlap running horizontally. This was nailed with galvanised nails onto 3x2 (75x50mm) sawn timbers. The barns have a much heavier structure as they have a heavy fibre/concrete roof so the frame has to be stronger. It is much easier to clad the sides before the roof goes on, *but* leave the wire front off until the very last.

Roof
There are two sorts of roofing material I recommend, which we have used since 1992. On our first two barns we used plastic-coated steel roofs, which are reasonably light in weight, but they are not good insulation. In hot weather the pens heat up and in cold weather not only is it cold but condensation drips down from the roof. By contrast, the fibre/concrete roofing material, which comes in several nice colours, as well as grey, is a very good insulator and so pens keep warmer in the winter and cooler in the summer, and better still they have 90 per cent less condensation. However, for small pens or for people who are just building one or two pens, this material is heavy and needs larger dimension timbers, making the pens more expensive.

As good, although not as structurally sound, is a roofing material called Onduline. We used it last year on the Small Falcon Block. It is lightweight and the company provides very good instructions on how to use it. It has a fifteen year guarantee. You

The Large Falcon Barn, showing the fibre concrete roof, bath doors and brick walls at the front

The Small Falcon and Hawk Aviaries, showing the Onduline roof

do need to put reasonably good support underneath it, but that goes for any lighter weight material. And being made of a paper-based material it is a very good insulator giving good winter and summer temperatures and it is not prone to condensation. My only complaint about it is that the clear sheets from Onduline (other makes won't fit the profile) are very expensive. I managed to get a more reasonable price because I was buying a reasonable quantity, but per single sheet they are bloody expensive. Any good DIY merchant should be able to get Onduline for you (see also Useful Addresses). Make sure that you do put enough light panels in to make the pen light and airy, but don't extend them over the service passage as this works better if it is dark.

Finishing

Once the roof is complete, the building is starting to look finished. You should have two doors, possibly three. We usually have one at either end of the service passage and if you have several aviaries in a line, this is a good idea. You can just have a bolt on the inside at the end that is not used much and this gives added security. The door to the pen is better if it opens outwards into the passage. Make sure that it will open all the way and lie flat against the inside passage wall so you can get past it easily. This door need have no lock, just a bolt or a catch as it is an internal door.

Feed Trays

If you are tethering your new birds straightaway, you are either going to throw food gently onto the ground next to the new bird, or try to feed it on the fist. If it is a hand-reared owl you will be going into the pen and hand-feeding it. But when you get to the stage of having your bird loose in the pen, there may be days when you just want to put food into the pen rather than feeding the bird on the fist. The same goes if you are putting the untrained bird in free for a month before starting training. We have found the best way to do this: using a jigsaw, cut an oblong hole in the back wall big enough to take a drawer-type feed ledge (ours are usually about 1ft (30cm) wide, 18in (45cm) long and 3in (7cm) deep. This gives the birds enough room to land and take the food. The ledge should be about 3ft (1m) off the ground, and is best situated near the corner of the back wall. Then just nail or screw a strut of timber across one corner of the inside of the pen at the back to support the drawer and make a drawer to fit. Either bevel the edges of the timber or pad them, so the landing place cannot cause foot damage. The drawer can then be removed and scrubbed regularly. It will open onto a dark passage and therefore the bird is very unlikely to try to get out of the hole while you are doing this. The feed tray keeps food off the ground, means you can easily see if the bird has left anything and generally works very well. During the period that the bird is tethered for training, or retraining, the tray can be taken out to prevent the bird trying to bate towards it.

Perches

Birds that are going to be tethered for a short while each year need perches that are easily removable. If you screw some wooden cups to the struts of your side walls you can then drop in a good perch pole. We suggest that you cover this pole with either Astroturf, natural fibre carpet or coconut door matting so that the bird has a good perch that will not cause bumblefoot. Two perches running the width of the pen is fine. We have just tried out an idea suggested by Dr Nick Fox. We put a high shelf perch at the back of our moulting pens (it is high enough so that tethered birds are not constantly bating trying to get there) and the birds love it. Ours is covered in carpet. It seems to work well and I thank Nick and Barbro for the suggestion, among others!

You need good perches, but you can't have them in the pen when the bird is tethered or she will be permanently wanting to sit on the higher perches rather than on the block or bow perch. So the perches must be easy to get in and out, and please remember that when you position the door from the passage into the pen itself! There is no reason why the perches shouldn't just be laid on the ground right at the front or back of the pen where they can't be hit by wings when bating. Once the bird is ready to go loose, you can place the perches close enough to the front so that your bird will land on them rather than hit the wire. At the same time place them far enough away from the wire or they will be hit by droppings. Follow the same principles with the back wall, and you will find the pen easier to clean.

Flooring

We have experimented with all sorts of materials over the years. Large-sized gravel is bad for feathers particularly when a bird is tethered, it is also very difficult to clean. Fine pea gravel is OK, but we tried it in the Hawk Walk in 92/93 and I didn't think it was better than sand and, indeed, it had two qualities that made it worse. In June 92 we did actually have some hot weather for a change. The pea gravel got so hot in the sun that it was not possible to touch it so that was obviously no good for tethered birds. In addition, birds that tended to bate more than usual, instead of just wearing their wing tips as would be the case on sand, the pea gravel caused 1in (3cm) chips of feather to break which was unacceptable.

Next year we are going to go back to sand as it seems to be the best material with the least problems. However, sand can get onto the food and can be swallowed. If you are going to have your bird loose in the pen once she is trained, then you will have either a feed drawer or ledge or perches good enough for the bird to sit on while feeding and so this problem will be minimal. Our tethered birds often have sand in their castings, but I have never had a problem. You can use any soft builders' sand, but if you use a very yellow or very red one, you will end up with a yellow or pink bird! The best sand to use is either silver sand, which is expensive unless you live near Leighton Buzzard as this is where it comes from, or dune sand. We get ours from a sand and dredging company near Cardiff but it should be available near most of the British coastline. It is nicely rounded, washed by the sea and works very well.

Soil is bad for feathers, gets very hard and dry, and if it is wet the birds can pick up parasitic infections particularly if they occasionally eat worms or small slugs. It is also very difficult to clean and I don't think it is acceptable as a surface.

Under *no circumstances* use any bark-like materials, shavings or sawdust. These can all harbour *Aspergillus* spores which, particularly with a young bird under stress during training, can kill in a matter of days.

Water

We are installing automatic cattle drinkers into all the compartments that house the trained, tethered birds because I don't think we offer birds water often enough. Although 99 per cent of the time they don't use it when it is there, they will have good clean fresh water available to drink. The drinkers should be too small for them to bathe in which is what we want. We offer the trained birds baths on a regular basis in the winter and every day in the summer.

If you are intending to keep your bird tethered then all you need do is give her a fresh moveable bath each day, making sure that you don't give it to a freshly tethered bird until she has learnt to sit on her perch. However, if you are going to have your bird loose once she is tame and trained, or you are going to have an owl which you are not going to tether anyway, a purpose-built bath as a part of the pen is a good idea. We build one into the centre of the low front wall, as a part of the wall, or more often afterwards. It really doesn't have to be tied in as there is no weight or pressure on it. We build it of brick to the same height as the front wall, either a square or an oblong, usually about 2ft (60cm) square unless it's a very large bird such as an eagle or one of the very big eagle owls, in which case it is 3ft (1m) square. Then the following day, when the brickwork has gone off and the mortar is dry, we fill the bath with rubble to

Laertes, a 1¹/₂-year-old Hybrid Saker/Peregrine having a bath

*A built-in corner bath – no good for eagles,
as their wing tips touch the wire*

A free-standing built-in bath

about 6in (15cm) below the top of the brickwork and then, with a damp mix of smooth concrete with some Unibond mixed in to make it waterproof, we shape a smooth base over the rubble and a curved 4in (10cm) wide edge over the surrounding brickwork. This gives a nice place for the birds to sit, it's good for their talons as it will wear them a little and it looks nice. When you build the frame for the wire on the front you make a smaller frame the length of the bath, giving you an opening about 4in (10cm) high with a door that opens outwards. In this way you can clean the bath from the outside and not disturb the bird in the moulting season. Put a small lock on that door for security. During the winter the bath will not need to be cleaned so often, but in the summer a quick scrub with a short-handled brush, a swill round and a refill every three days will stop it from going green. If it freezes in the winter it is probably too cold for the birds to bath anyway so don't worry but if, like us, you have put in an automatic drinker on the back wall, you will find that this is unlikely to freeze in all but the severest of weather. Don't forget to insulate the pipework well.

If you don't want to make a fixed bath then you can just buy the normal hawk's bath from a falconry furniture manufacturer. Make sure you place it away from perches so that droppings don't fall straight in and empty, clean and fill it regularly. Personally I prefer the built-in bath as it means it can be filled at any time of year without needing to go into the pen. So if you happen to be away and someone else is looking after your bird, there is less chance of them letting it out by accident and less disturbance to the bird.

Now we have a nearly completed pen, with four walls, three of them solid, one unfinished, and a rear or side entrance passage, all totally roofed in with plenty of shelter and light; well-built doors with room to get in and out; a concrete passage for easy comfortable access and cleaning; a nice sandy floor about 5in (13cm) deep, and a bath, a feed drawer, and perches available and ready with cups to hold them, but not yet up, except for young owls. The outside of the pen has been tidied up and preferably has a strip of gravel at least 1ft (30cm) along the walls, and there should be a decent path leading to the pen. The gutters have been put on and all the water has drained away to a drain, or pond, or large soakaway.

Wire Mesh

The frame is ready for the wire and once that is up the pen is finished. I would recommend using any of the welded mesh-type wire and I would suggest that whatever the bird, you use either 1in (25mm) square mesh or 1x2in (25x50mm), the reason being that rats and birds cannot easily get through 1in (25mm) mesh and so your bird will not come into contact with either. One of the added advantages of a solid roof over your bird is that wild bird droppings cannot get into the pen from small birds sitting above or flying over as they would in an open-topped pen, only covered in wire. The diseases that birds of prey can get are often found in other birds, including sparrows, starlings, pigeons and the like. The less contamination that you ensure for your bird the better and that includes avoiding contamination through droppings into drinking water or onto food.

Some people may think that I am being over-cautious here, but you would be amazed what infections apparently healthy small wild birds have. We did some filming in Scotland with a Merlin and the director asked for the bird to be eating a wild quarry species. So the film people provided a freshly killed sparrow, and within two days of eating it the Merlin showed signs of illness. After he had been driven from the north of Scotland to Stroud on a non-stop drive to get him to the vets he died, on arrival, from an infection directly received from the sparrow. So be warned and avoid this by learning from our experiences.

Maintenance

Once you have the wire stapled on we suggest painting it matt black as it looks so much nicer and is far easier to see through. You can either use a black bitumen paint (but be prepared to ruin the roller) or we use black emulsion. It tends to wear off whatever it is and we paint the wire on our pens every year. The emulsion is easier to use, doesn't ruin clothing or rollers and the bitumen wears out just as quickly so you have little advantage.

We also 'Timbercare' all the pens every year mainly for cosmetic reasons but also to maintain the timber in good condition. After all this effort it is a shame to let the standard of the pen go downhill.

The pen described will suit most birds, though there may be some variations with the more nervous or difficult species which I will discuss in Part II.

Shed/Indoor Quarters

No matter how good your aviary there may come a time when you need to have a bird confined inside. She could have been injured while out hunting, she could get an infection that requires warmth and antibiotics twice a day. There are many unforeseen things that can happen to livestock, usually at the most inconvenient times and almost always on a Bank Holiday Sunday!

You will also need somewhere to store food and the very smart collecting box you built to get your bird in the first place (see page 55). Your equipment, such as weighing machine, gloves, bags etc, will also need to be stored somewhere. So it is best to have either a room in the house, if you have a spare one, or an insulated shed perhaps even as a part of the aviary. In here you will need a deep freeze for a good stock of food, and various other pieces of equipment including a night quarter. This is a solid box large enough for the bird to sit in comfortably with a door with vertical bars on.

Weighing Room

Our weighing room which contains most of what an individual bird of prey keeper should need is about 12x8ft (3.6x2.4m) and this would be big enough for most people. There is no window, except for a glass panel in the door, and this is covered on the inside by vertical bamboo. If a bird is difficult and starts flying round the room, she can't hurt herself on the glass.

The door to your weighing room must have a good bolt on the inside and you must make it an *unbreakable habit* to close the door and bolt it if you have the bird with you. A bolt may seem old fashioned as you could put a Yale lock on, but the action of locking the bolt will always remind you of the dangers of losing birds by being careless. I have been closing the door on our weighing room and locking the rather nice brass bolt for twenty-six years now and I never fail to be reminded of what can happen should someone unexpectedly open the door while I am weighing the bird or whatever.

I would suggest that you have an old (or new if you like) chest of drawers and then you will have plenty of space to put spare leashes, your creance, dummy rabbit, spare bits of leather, engineering files for beaks, electrical wire cutters for coping, telemetry and so on. If you are going to keep any spare wings for lures put them in mothballs as they will get eaten.

You will need a deep freeze for storing food, we have a fridge as well as we are flying many birds each day and so need a fair amount of meat out. But for only one bird, you can probably get away without one as long as you freeze the different types of food in small portions.

You will need a table or worktop to cut meat and it is sensible to have a cutting board to save the surface of the table and so that you can clean it daily. We have a sink with hot and cold water so that we can wash leashes, blocks, cutting boards etc. But a bucket of hot water brought from the house would probably do. Cleanliness is very important with the care of any animal, but particularly a meat-eater, as meat can go off very quickly and bugs can grow. Falconry bags, gloves and the like should be kept clean, or at least cleaned on a regular basis and I don't mean regularly once a year!

A wall cupboard for emergency medical supplies is very useful because, as I said before, birds always get ill or injured at the most inconvenient moments. This should be lockable to stop children getting at anything that might harm them. You should keep any disinfectants in there as well.

Some people like to have a daybook where they chart down the weight of their bird and her daily behaviour. We have a blackboard on the wall in our weighing room and the bird's weight is written down each day of the week, with a column for the name of the bird, a column for the flying weight (if known) and seven columns for the days of the week. The last column is available for comments – rude or otherwise!

A few hooks to hang bags, gloves, coats etc, are very useful. For those who might be spending a great deal of time in the weighing room with their bird, a chair is nice so that you and your bird can relax – the dog can always sit in it when you are not using it!

Installing electricity and water to your shed/weighing room would make sense. The only safe form of immediate heating in such a room, which might house a bird, is electric heating as all other forms such as gas or oil bring with them the danger of fumes. Just a warning about fumes at this point might be useful. Last year we had a bird killed on a film set because the scenery caught fire and myself and the bird were enveloped in polystyrene fumes for a couple of minutes. The bird died, showing no clinical signs until it was too late, two days later. Neil Forbes, our vet, pointed out that birds are very much more susceptible to fumes than other species which is why canaries were used in mines to detect gas. A non-stick pan overheating or burning is lethal to birds and Neil has known all the pet birds in a block of flats to be killed by such an incident. Be aware of this fact when having a bird in the house.

We probably have more equipment than the average falconer!

BIRD	FLYING WEIGHT	MO	TU	WE	TH	FR	SA	SU	NOTES
CHALKY	4.4	4.4	4.5	4.4	4.4	/	4.5	4.5	
ANDROMEDA	6.6	6.8	6.9	6.8	6.7	6.8	6.6	6.6	
ATALANTA	1.15	/	/	1.15	2.0	2.1	2.0	1.15½	
BILBERRY	1.5	/	/	1.6	1.6½	1.6	1.5½	/	
STORMFORCE	2.0	2.0	2.½	/	/	2.0	2.1	2.1	
MIKE	1.6	1.6	1.6	1.7	1.6½	/	/	1.6	
ALISON	1.14½	1.15	1.14	/	1.15	1.15	2.0	1.15½	
TOUCH&GO	3.7	3.7	/	/	/	3.7	3.7½	3.7	
BINGLE	3.4	/	/	3.4	3.4	/	/	3.4	

Our weight board

CHAPTER THREE
FALCONRY FURNITURE AND EQUIPMENT

What you need will depend on why you have a bird, what you are doing with her and on the species. For those who are just keeping a bird but not training or handling her, you don't need much in the way of equipment. I would suggest that you still need the indoor quarters as you still need to store and prepare food and there is just as much chance an aviary bird may become sick as one that is trained and flown.

Non-flying Aviary Birds

You need a good net and a good falconry glove.

You should catch your bird at least once a year to give her a physical checkover and to move her to your smart holding box so that you can give the aviary a good clean with disinfectant. The easiest and least traumatic way to catch up a bird is with a net. Any good fishing shop should sell them. You want a large size with soft mesh, preferably small holes and the net must be at least 2ft (60cm) deep. Birds bounce out of a shallow net. You will also need a decent glove as picking up birds of prey or owls without a glove is very stupid and potentially painful!

Flying and Handled Birds

Scales
This is a vital piece of equipment for all birds being handled and trained. *A decent weighing machine* can be either modern electrical scales or the old type of balance scales, which I prefer. I have known people use kitchen spring-balance scales that are designed for weighing cooking materials: they must be insane as these are notoriously inaccurate.

Remember whatever you use, *inaccurate scales can, have and will kill*. We have a pair of old balance shop scales, modified to take the birds. You just change the pan for a comfortable perch for the bird, and check that it balances well without weights. As long as the scales balance freely and evenly, with no bird on them, and the weights are good, then you can't go wrong. We check them with a known weight on a regular basis. I am not that confident with the modern electrical scales; we have a set that we use when taking the birds away, but I just don't trust them. Unless you test them regularly with a known weight you don't know when they are reading inaccurately. I like the old balance scales that you used to see in greengrocers. You can buy these new at kitchen shops, but don't get the weights unless they have the government stamp on the base. The best place to get weights is from a firm called Avery Scales.

An important point to remember with weighing birds is that you should always use your weighing machine; your commonsense and your hands, ie you should feel the body condition of the bird every day as well as weighing her. This entails gently placing your hand under the feathers of the breast and feeling the meat on the breast bone and under the wings. This will indicate the condition of the bird, whether she is fat or thin, whether the muscle is soft or hard. But remember different species will have different shaped breast bones: a Peregrine has a very deep breast bone, with plenty of muscle for long periods of fast flying; owls tend to have a much shallower breast bone. The right amount of flesh on the breast bone of a Peregrine could equate to an owl close to starvation and death.

Buzzards, Harris Hawks, True Hawks and Eagles

Scales
Vital for all groups of birds of prey being flown.

Gloves
Single thickness will do fine for small hawks such as Sparrowhawks or male Cooper's Hawks. Double thickness is necessary for the buzzards, Harrises and large hawks such as Goshawks. An eagle glove tends to be specially made. We cheat a little, and Martin Jones is going to hate me for this, but for eagles I like to use what is called an overlay glove. It is a single or double glove with a thumb but no fingers, the end is just open and you can use a small glove inside. They are less bulky than a special eagle glove and because you have a thin glove underneath, your fingers are freer and more able to deal with jesses, leashes and the like. I know Martin hates making them but they are really very good and I always use them when I can persuade him or his excellent staff to produce them for me. They are fairly expensive, but I have had one for fifteen years now so the outlay is worth it.

Good gloves are expensive, but they should last you for years if they are looked after properly. It always make me laugh quietly to myself when I see someone with a gorgeous bird on their fist, sitting on an old welding glove or something similar. It doesn't show much pride in the bird. Mind you some people go too far the other way and have such ornate gloves that they look ridiculous. Martin Jones makes the best gloves I have seen or used right across the falconry world and that includes Europe, Africa and North America.

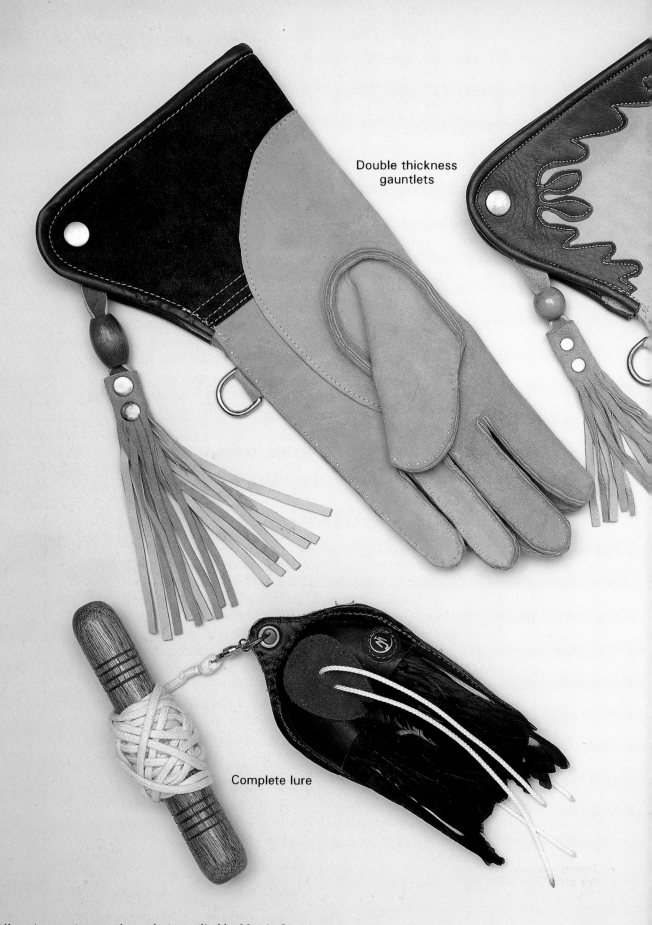

Double thickness
gauntlets

Complete lure

All equipment (except the scales) supplied by Martin Jones at
Falconry Furniture (see list of suppliers for address and telephone number)

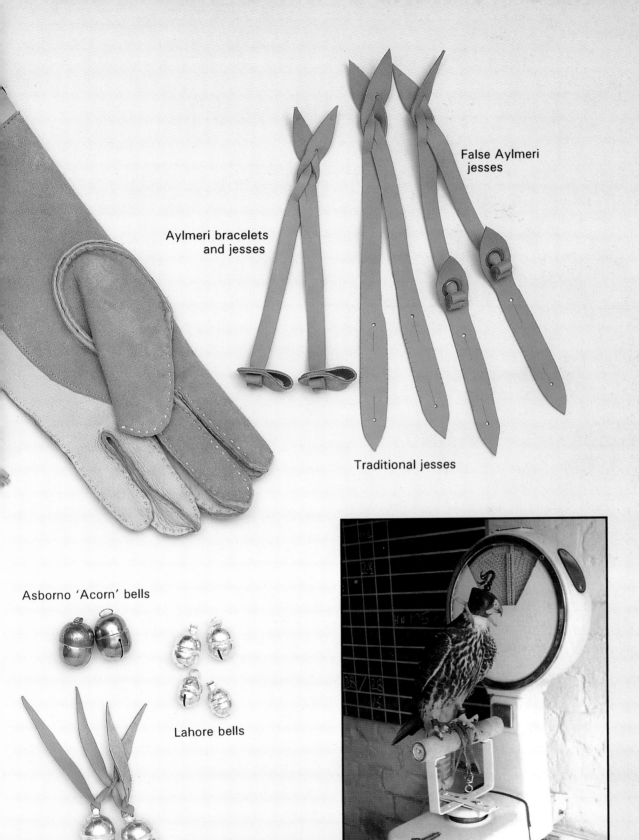

Aylmeri bracelets and jesses

False Aylmeri jesses

Traditional jesses

Asborno 'Acorn' bells

Lahore bells

Traditional bewitts for attaching bells to birds' legs

Scales

All equipment should be kept neatly. The two gloves on the left are overlay gloves

A Bow Perch

The leather-topped padded ones are better than the bound rope ones. The good leather ones have a leather top bound over a polystyrene-type pipe lagging. They are softer and particularly suited to Sparrowhawks and Black Sparrowhawks which are more prone to bumblefoot than the other hawk, buzzard or eagle species. Martin, from whom we get all our equipment here at The National Birds of Prey Centre, makes a rather good bow perch that can have either heavyweight metal feet for indoors, or screw-in spikes for outdoors. This gives you the best of both worlds without needing two perches. A leather-padded perch, such as those we use, is not suitable for use where it is not under a shelter. If allowed to get wet on a regular basis the leather will go very hard and shiny. In this case I would probably use a rope-bound perch, but then I don't leave tethered birds where they can get wet very often and I wouldn't advise others to do it either.

Once a bird is really tame, and if she is not going to be let loose in a pen which is the preferred method of keeping birds, then we sometimes put a large log or rock by the bow perch, so that the bird has two choices of perching places. It should be placed so that the bird can reach it easily, but not get the other side of it, and away from the direction from which you would normally approach the bird so that should she bate towards you, she will not hit wings or tail on the stone. These work particularly well for eagles who might naturally be sitting on much larger objects than a bow perch. Large eagles may not be able to sit on the leather-padded perch as strong talons may rip the leather, in which case a rope-bound one will do the trick.

Jesses

Always buy two pairs for one bird so that you have a spare pair in stock. Aylmeri jesses are the best; these are a leather bracelet held together with an eyelet, then a strap is threaded through and the swivel attached to that. They were invented by a man called Guy Aylmer, hence the name, and there are the most amazing pronunciations these days! The only thing you have to watch with Aylmeri is jess sores on the top of the back toe. These will develop if the eyelet is too big, if there is not enough leather surrounding the eyelet or if the bird tends to bate a lot. None of these factors are a problem if you are keeping your bird loose in a nice pen rather than tethering her. If your bird does start to get red patches behind the back toe you should get her checked by the vet. We then put Elastoplast bandages under the jesses if we can see a problem starting, change the jesses and keep an eye on the toe. If there are actual open sores or scabs you have no alternative but to let the bird loose, untethered, until the sores heal properly and this can take several weeks.

While the bird is tethered for initial training or retraining you will have what are called mews jess straps through the eyelet. These have a slot which goes through and over the swivel. Some people have slotless straps that they use when going hunting, removing the mews jesses and replacing them with field jesses. The whole point of this is to avoid a bird getting tangled up by the jesses, should the slot get caught up in a twig, branch, bramble or barbed wire. We use a slightly different method; we have two very thin, probably only ⅛in (3mm) wide, strips of strong leather which are attached to the eyelets at all times. They are attached by looping through and

LEFT *An outdoor bow perch. The top is padded with leather, which I prefer*
RIGHT *An indoor/outdoor bow perch. Note the bath is positioned to one side so that it does not catch the bird's droppings*

around the eyelet a couple of times. They are narrow enough not to get in the way of the mews jesses and long enough to allow you to hold onto to your bird but there is almost no possibility of them getting caught up. They will also not get pulled out and generally they are a better alternative to field jesses.

I have been against what are called 'False Aylmeri' in the past because birds can get their back talon caught in the eyelet. We have had problems with true Aylmeri and don't feel we can go on using traditional jesses, so this year we are going back to False Aylmeri and I hope they will work for us. For those of you who are sensible and train your bird to work from an aviary you will not have a problem with jess sores, because these only happen on tethered birds. Traditional jesses are no longer favoured because there is always a risk of a bird getting tangled in thick cover with a twig getting caught through the slots. I have known a falcon catch the slot of a traditional jess on the barb of a barbed-wire fence, but I have known the same thing happen to the slotless removable hunting jess. I think that the very thin permanent straps that we have on our birds don't hold the same risk.

Whatever you decide to use, all jesses should be checked and greased on a daily basis. The leather of the mews straps should be checked daily as the only places they wear are just below the knot and at the slots. As you soften the jesses with grease, pretty much on a daily basis, you will be able to check all your equipment at the same time. We use a grease called Ko-cho-line which is available from saddlery shops and is excellent. When resting a bird and not flying her, perhaps for moulting, remove all jesses and replace with new ones for the next season. Don't trust old, worn jesses.

Swivels

You should always have at least two of these, because they are the easiest piece of equipment to lose. This is also a vital piece of falconry furniture, because if this breaks and your bird is not kept safely in an aviary, not only have you had it because you have lost your bird, but the bird is at risk because the jesses are fastened together on the swivel and the bird will get tangled and die. If you are not prepared to pay good money for a decent swivel you should not even be considering getting a bird.

Leash

Gone are the days when people use leather leashes. If you see anyone still using one, they must be mentally deficient. Leather leashes can break without showing any signs of wear, and not to use modern materials for leashes in this day and age is insane. Braided Terylene is strong, easy to tie, shows signs when starting to wear and comes in quite pretty colours. The leash should have a good solid knot at the end, with the end melted over the knot. It is probably a good idea to have one with a leather washer on the end as well. You can also get a flat style Terylene leash with a traditional button end instead of a figure-of-eight knot. I always find these slightly less easy to tie, but it really makes no difference which type you choose as long as you get one, or better still two, as it is advisable to have a spare.

Bells

There are lots of different types of bells made in various countries including the UK. The best I have seen are the Steve Little bells made in the USA, but again it really doesn't matter as long as the bell is not too large and heavy for the bird and rings well. Go to a reputable supplier and don't get a bell for a small falcon or hawk that would be more suited to a Rottweiler!

We tend to use tail bells a great deal here, for every different group of birds that we bell. They ring better, can be heard from further away and last longer. But if I was hunting with most of the larger hawks and buzzards, and even eagles, I would have one or two leg bells as well as the tail bell.

Under no circumstances should the bell be attached to the bird's leg with cable ties. I have actually seen birds with bells put directly onto the leg with cable ties, this is madness as the plastic can badly damage the bird's leg. I have also seen bells fixed to the closed ring with cable ties and to the eyelet of the Aylmeri jesses. None of these ways are acceptable and all can, and have, injured birds.

The traditional ways of fitting bells are the best and the safest. I know it takes longer to fit a tail bell with leather straps and glue, but using cable ties has killed at least one bird I know of. If a bird really hates a tail bell, she pulls at the bell with her beak. I know of a Harris Hawk that did this, got her beak trapped under the cable tie and drowned in her own bath. The old method means that if a bird really hates the bell (and it is unusual but does happen occasionally) she can pull it off without injuring herself.

The same goes for leg bells, a nice old-fashioned leather bewitt strap (the leather strap that keeps the bell on) holds the bell well away from the leg. The material used is soft against the bird's leg and the system has been tried and tested for centuries. Some modern changes are a good thing, but change for the sake of change with no good reason other than making life easier is just not a good idea.

Creance

This is a training line usually 30–55yd (25–50m) long. There is no need to have one any longer as by the time the bird is flying to you over that length readily, then it is time for her to go loose anyway. Strong braided Terylene is the best material, wound onto a nice stick in a figure-of-eight pattern as this is the best way to keep the line tidy. Several words of warning though:

- Always have control of the end of your line, either tie it to yourself, your bag or your glove, then you will not be chasing after it should the bird decide it's time to fly past you and into a tree.
- If a bird does fly past your raised fist, and gets up speed, you will need to bring her down gently, that is why I don't suggest that you fix the creance to the ground. If it is on a part of your clothing or equipment then you can physically move and cushion the bird's arrival at the end of the line.
- Don't try to slow the bird and the line down with your bare hand – you will get very bad burns from a fast-moving creance. Just to give you an example, I was flying a young African Fish Eagle on a line at a show and the wind took her up, I had to bring her down inside the ring and because of unforeseen circumstances I had no assistant that day. I missed the line with my gloved hand, only holding it with my bare hand and I knew, long before the eagle hit the end of the line it was going to hurt. I had burns going into my fingers at the joints that were through to the bone and took

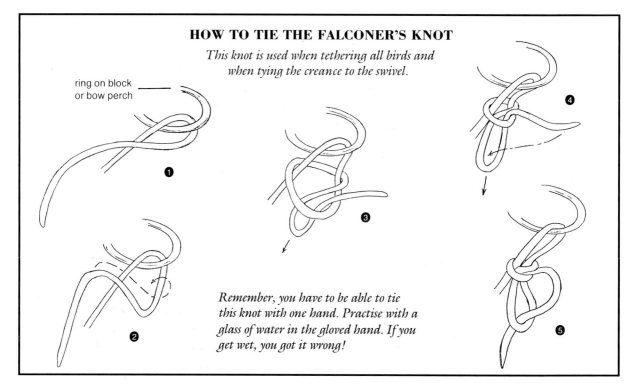

HOW TO TIE THE FALCONER'S KNOT

This knot is used when tethering all birds and when tying the creance to the swivel.

ring on block or bow perch

Remember, you have to be able to tie this knot with one hand. Practise with a glass of water in the gloved hand. If you get wet, you got it wrong!

weeks to heal. Far more painful and slow healing than if I had been bitten or grabbed by the bird itself – so be warned and be careful.

● Get a good strong line because if your training line breaks you and the bird are in big trouble.

Rabbit Lure (Dummy Bunny)

In Britain it is totally illegal to use bagged or caught live quarry to enter a bird of prey to hunting. So if any of you have read old books or talked to uninformed people on the subject of getting birds actually to hunt and have been told this is the way to do it, get it out of your mind instantly. Not only is it illegal, but if anyone were stupid enough to do it they would put the sport of falconry at risk. Anyone who says that you can't get a bird hunting without using bagged quarry is a complete prat and should not be allowed to have a bird.

Buy or make yourself a nice dummy bunny. These days synthetic fur is better and lasts longer and it should have a place to tie on a piece of meat. It will also be much better if it has a nice pulling line on a handle similar to that on a decent falcon lure.

Bath

Even if you have a built-in bath in your aviary, it is not a bad idea to have a bath so that if you go away you can take it with you for the bird. The bath should be large enough for the bird to have a comfortable amount of room for her size, with a nice rounded lip for the bird to sit on, but without any protuberances for a leash to catch on. It should not be any deeper than 5in (12cm) at the most for large birds and 2½in (6cm) for small birds.

Falconry Bag

The important thing about falconry bags is that they must have at least two deep pockets: one for dummy rabbit/lures/quarry; and one for the meat used to call the bird to the fist. They must also be made of a material which is easily disinfected. You could use any sort of canvas bag that will fit these specifications, but quite frankly a properly designed and made falconry/hawking bag is far better in the long run.

Some people prefer to use a jacket; I have not really tried to use one for any length of time, but as long as they have the same specifications as described above it really doesn't matter if it is a bag or a jacket. I have found, however, that the jackets can be quite difficult to use as they tend to ride up when you are trying to get anything out of the pockets and any pockets on the left side are pretty useless if you are trying to get stuff out with only your right hand.

Hood

I have to admit that I am at a loss as to what to tell you here. We are talking about the buzzard and hawk family at the moment and we don't hood any of ours. I do not approve of any species going out hunting with other birds, except Harris Hawks, therefore you do not need a hood to stop your Red-tail or Common Buzzard or Goshawk seeing other birds fly which is the main use of a hood for a falcon. In this day and age of vandalism and theft I would strongly advise people to use travelling boxes for their birds so that they are safe and cannot be seen from the outside of a car or van, so you don't need a hood to travel the bird. The more a hawk/buzzard gets to see in the way of people, dogs, tractors, prams, and anything else that might crop up in her life, the tamer and happier the bird will be and the less chance you have of losing her. Hoods are often misused and left on birds for too long or used to make the bird quiet when in fact she should be unhooded and be getting tame. If I were you I would not buy a hood for a hawk or *buteo* and I certainly would not put one on a Sparrowhawk. The only possible exception to this rule might be a Black Sparrowhawk but, as this book is for beginners, don't even let that species enter your mind!

If you do decide to get a hood for a *buteo* or hawk then Anglo-Indian hoods tend to be the cheaper option and fit the hawks and buzzards better. Much the same applies to eagles with an added warning: hooded eagles can snatch out with their feet and if they do make contact with any part of your anatomy while hooded it will be very, very painful. They will not let go until unhooded, so if you have to hood an eagle: *take great care.*

Travelling Box for all Diurnal Birds of Prey

There are many factors to be taken into account when travelling your bird: you may need to travel on a daily basis to fly your bird away from home; you may just want to go places at the weekend. If you intend hunting you will have to travel to the various farms where you have permission to fly.

We used just to put a bird in the back of the car or van either on an indoor bow perch or block or cadge, or on a car perch on the back of the passenger seat. I would not dare do that now. There are so many people who are either anti-birds in captivity, or who would consider stealing the bird, or even those who are just vandals, that it is

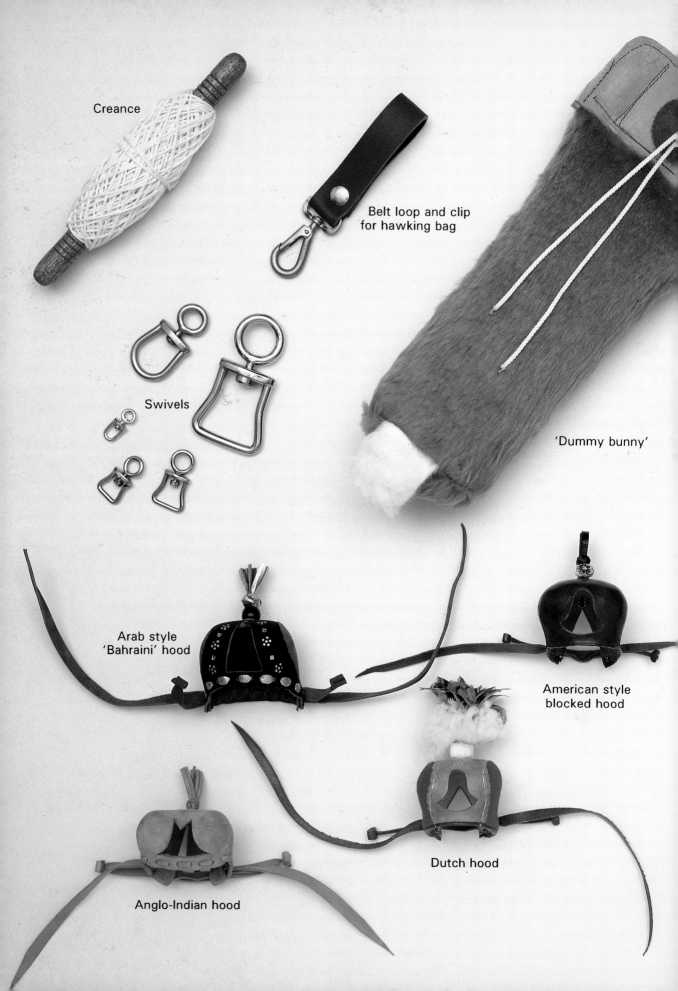

Creance

Belt loop and clip
for hawking bag

Swivels

'Dummy bunny'

Arab style
'Bahraini' hood

American style
blocked hood

Dutch hood

Anglo-Indian hood

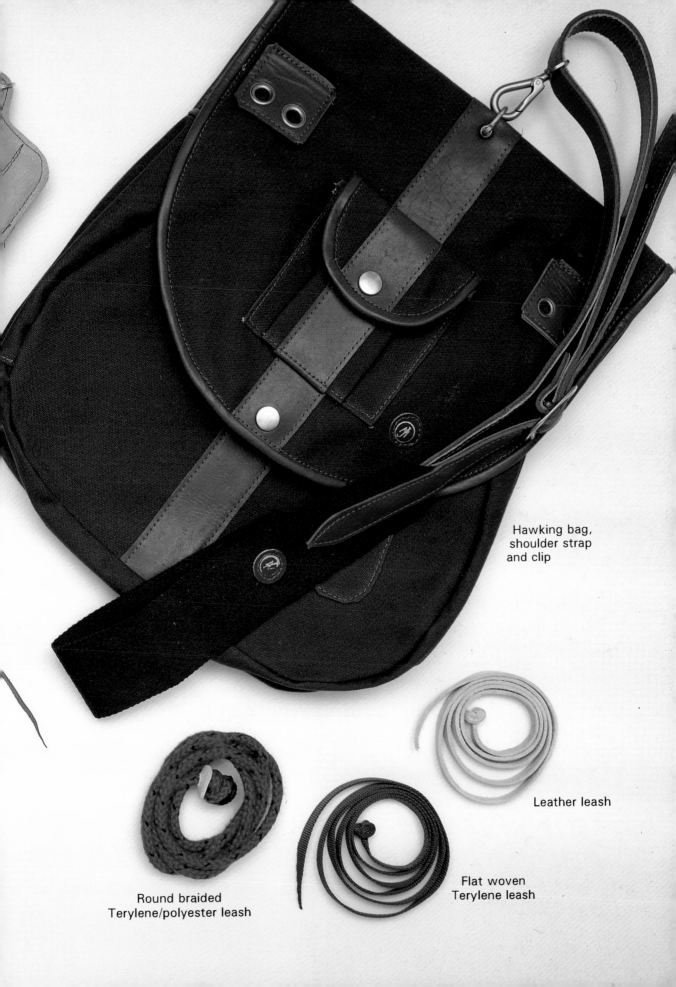

Hawking bag,
shoulder strap
and clip

Leather leash

Flat woven
Terylene leash

Round braided
Terylene/polyester leash

asking for trouble to leave a bird in sight of anyone who might look inside your car. I don't like leaving hooded birds unattended so we have a vehicle that is kitted out inside for the birds. I have been travelling all sorts of different birds to flying demonstrations at shows for the last twenty-six years. We have made numerous sets of boxes and I think we have just about got it right. You don't need to build a set like mine, but you should have one box for your bird to travel safely and comfortably, out of sight of prying eyes, unhooded and in no danger.

We build a box large enough for the falcon, hawk, eagle or buzzard to sit in on a perch so that she can turn around, hop onto the floor, or back onto the perch without hitting her head or damaging her tail. But do be careful not to build a beautiful box, perfect for your bird, and then find it will not fit into your car! We have a wooden perch of 2x1in (50x25mm) timber, covered in natural fibre carpet, that slots into a wooden cup screwed onto the side of the box. The box is built of ¾in (15mm) blockboard so you don't need a frame because the wood is strong enough in its own right. The door opens like a cupboard door and is just about the full size of the box. We put newspaper on the floor below the perch and usually drill some ventilation holes around the bottom of the box. You will find that once a bird knows that this is home after being flown she will be eager to get back in there. I usually feed my demonstration birds in there on the way home so that they are kept occupied. Our newest boxes are stained and varnished as the older white ones made one of my birds too active inside the box because of the light colour.

We are actually going to put small lights into each box so that we can let the birds feed more easily, particularly when the birds are away for several days at a time. These boxes then work very well as night quarters for the birds and this means if we are staying at hotels, or camping, we know the birds are warm and safe. You do have to be careful though, because if the sun is hot early in the day then the vehicle must be parked in good shade to prevent the boxes from heating up and killing the birds.

This design is not suitable for untrained birds as it is too difficult to get them out easily, which is why we have the box with the sliding door for owls and untrained birds, see Chapter 4.

Chalky in his travelling box. This is for the trained birds only, ie not untrained or sick ones

Falcons

Scales
Vital for all groups of birds of prey being flown.

Glove
A single thickness is fine for any of the falcons.

A Block
Falcons being birds that would be more likely to sit on rocks or posts than in trees have traditionally been kept on blocks rather than bow perches and they do better on them. There is only one type of block worth using and that is what Martin Jones calls the European-style block. This has a block of turned wood with a long spike, part of which is above the ground and part below. The older 'traditional blocks' have the wooden block going right down to the ground. The former type is preferred because very occasionally a falcon can straddle a block, ie, the jesses slip down either side if they have stretched a little. If this happens a bird can injure herself internally on the old type if her body is pulled up tight against the wooden part of the block. If the jesses are caught around only the thin metal spike of the European-style block, the only thing that can get damaged is her tail which is not a problem.

The top surface of the block is very important: really you only have two choices. Astroturf is the most popular and is generally very good, but if you don't keep it very clean, particularly with Lanners and Luggers, you will get foot problems. It should be cleaned every day. We have a deep cork top on all the blocks except those used for Gyrs which do better on Astroturf. Cork is warm in winter, cool in summer, easy to clean and disinfect. But it has to be at least 1½in (4cm) deep so that the top can be made uneven with a surform file. Thin cork is not good enough. I would recommend either but would suggest that for Lanners and Luggers, cork is better.

Jesses
We recommend Aylmeri or False Aylmeri. See pages 41-2.

Swivels
See page 42. Swivels are the same for every type of bird except that they are made in different sizes.

Leashes, Bells, Creance
See pages 42-4.

Lure
If you are flying Sakers or possibly New Zealand Falcons or Prairie Falcons, ie any of the falcons that take ground game, a dummy bunny is very useful as well.

I use a very simple lure, it's just a pair of wings, usually Magpie, Moorhen or Partridge, with a piece of meat. Tie the wings together back to back, with a piece of meat then tied to the wings. It's the line that is important: unless you have a line made of braided cotton you will damage your hands.

Complete lures, which have a leather pad made in the shape of a horseshoe, are not recommended. Some falcons can hit the lure very hard indeed and these leather pads can hurt a bird. They are also very hard to swing accurately. By making up a new lure every day, you ensure the safety of the lure line and of your bird.

Bath and Falconry Bag
See information on pages 44-5.

Hood
Falcons were probably the only birds in the past to be taken out in groups to go hunting and flown one at a time in turn. The hood, therefore, became a vital piece of equipment to stop those waiting falcons being upset by seeing the one being flown. The hood just calms a bird down. It is not an aid to training, it does not get a bird tame and it should not be over-used. The old-school falconers thought nothing of leaving a bird hooded for days at a time, only unhooding her to get her to feed. This is archaic thinking and does the bird no good. So when you buy a hood for a falcon don't over-use it.

Small falcons such as Merlins and the like do not need to be hooded. Only the larger falcons need a hood and only then where there is a good reason for it. Always buy a good hood that fits well. The best way to get a really well-fitting hood is to go to the hood-maker and try the hood on there and then, but this is rarely possible. However, good hood-makers will have a variety of sizes available and can exchange hoods that do not fit if they are returned immediately and in good condition. My favourite hoods are the American-style blocked hoods. The Americans have really worked on their hood-making and the good hood-makers over there are first class. Martin Jones was taught by Doug Pineo who makes lovely hoods and I get mine from Martin – when I can!

Owls

Scales
Scales are as important for the owls as for any other group, particularly the small owls.

Glove
For small to medium owls, and remember that I do not recommend small owls such as Barn Owls particularly for beginners, a single thickness glove is fine. We fly three Bengals which are the species we recommend for beginners and I use a small single thickness glove for them with no problems. For the Large Eagle Owls such as the European and the Great Horned Owl you will need a double-thickness glove as they are very powerful indeed when they do decide to grip.

A Bow Perch
Owls should not be tethered. If you get the right owl, at the right stage of her life, you will never need to tether her. Our Bengals were trained in their pens and have never sat on a bow perch or block. However, if you do need to tether an owl for a short period perhaps to disinfect or repair the pen, then a bow perch is better than a block.

Owls perch naturally with two toes forward and two back very often. Their feet are not that well adapted for flat surfaces (apart from the Snowy Owl which spends most of her time on the ground or at low levels – no trees where Snowies live!). They are happier sitting on branch-like perches.

Large owls should have large bow perches, a European Eagle Owl has feet not much smaller than a male Golden Eagle. Small owls should have Sparrowhawk-sized bow perches.

Jesses

Aylmeri bracelets, with a permanently fixed thin strap for holding your owl when going from the aviary to the weighing room or travelling box should you be going out to fly, are recommended. If you are a beginner then have the mews straps ready and use those as well, along with a leash and swivel. Don't forget: change the jesses at least once a year including the bracelets as these will get hard and worn.

Swivel

In the early stages of learning to handle an owl it is probably a good idea to put the mews straps on the Aylmeri bracelets and then the swivel and leash so that should the bird bate while on the fist you will not let her go by accident. Sparrowhawk and Merlin swivels are fine for small owls; large falcon size will fit medium owls such as Bengals and Savigny's and Magellans; Red-tail size is OK for the large owls such as Iranian, Turkmanian or European.

Leash

The sizes of leashes, for different species of owls, will match those described above for swivels.

Bells

We don't put bells on our owls here at The National Birds of Prey Centre, but we are flying them in the same place every day and on the very few times they have gone out of the flying field, every crow, rook and magpie has mobbed them and told us where they are. Also, being hand-reared they call to us which is almost as good as a bell. However, if you are going to fly an owl away from your home it is a good idea to put a bell or two on the bird and again the corresponding sizes for swivels will do for bells also.

Creance
See pages 43-4.

Rabbit Lure

It is quite a good idea to get the medium and large owls to chase one of these. If you are intending to hunt with an owl it is a very important part of the training as with the *buteos* and the hawks. If you are only flying an owl for fun, then it makes things a little more interesting for the owl and gives you another way to get your bird to come down out of a tree should she be a little slow! For the small owls you should be able to make yourself a dummy rat to interest them and amuse yourself.

Falcony Bag
See page 45.

Hood
You can't be serious! Believe it or not friends who work with Martin Jones tell me that they occasionally have a request for a hood for an owl. I find it hard to believe there are people who use so little of their brains, in fact in these cases the owl probably beats the owner for intelligence and I consider owls to be as thick as two short planks! *Please*, if you are considering taking up keeping or training any bird of prey or owl, remember you have what is supposed to be the most intelligent brain of any animal on this planet: *use it*. Think and use commonsense before asking any questions, some of the answers are so obvious that it seriously worries me when such questions are asked in the first place! By all means ask questions – that is the only way to learn – but think before you ask.

General Tools

Over the years you will find that you build up a collection of tools and equipment that you need for handling, training and flying birds of prey:
- Small electrical wire clippers for beaks and talons.
- Small engineering files for beaks.
- Leather punch for jesses.
- Aylmeri kit.
- Long-nosed pliers.
- A decent knife.
- A whistle (you should be ashamed of yourself if you can't whistle without one!)
- Glue: Rapid Araldite.
- Cutting board.
- Leather scissors or scalpel.
- A good net.

Keep all the equipment you need in your weighing room and keep it clean and tidy. Then when you need things in a hurry you will know where to find them.

Telemetry

Falconry survived without telemetry for thousands of years and many people can't afford a set. However, if you are going to fly the true hawks, eagles or falcons then you should have a set, it is pretty useful for hunting with owls as well. Generally the owls, buzzards and Harris Hawks are less likely to go long distances and if you have done your job properly then most of these are pretty difficult to lose. But if you can afford telemetry for these, your life will be made easier if they kill out of sight.

Goshawk fliers should definitely have telemetry. Goshawks have a tendency for self-hunting and can have the odd day when they seem to forget they are a trained bird and are supposed to come back to you when called. The use of telemetry has meant that Goshawks are flown at a higher weight and this is better for the bird, better for hunting and better for falconry in general.

I think I would probably not bother with telemetry for Sparrowhawks. They are not expensive to buy, they will survive in the wild if lost and as they should only be flown by experienced falconers, losing them should be less of a problem. For other *accipiters* such as Black Sparrowhawks, definitely use telemetry.

Some people use telemetry on Merlins, but it has to be of a small size. Merlins tend to fly relatively close to the falconer unless ringing up after a lark so actually a good pair of binoculars is probably of more use than telemetry.

Beginners should not be flying Kestrels and more experienced falconers are unlikely to want one. I would not bother with telemetry with these birds.

Large falcons are the long-distance travellers and telemetry has found many a lost bird for falconers all over the world. It is unwise to fly larger falcons without telemetry.

Eagles should really only be flown in open countryside and if used for hunting they can go a very long way, so telemetry is a must!

What Sort of Telemetry to Buy

Telemetry in the UK has improved immeasurably in the last few years. The most important thing to look at when buying telemetry is the after-sales service. Will it be mended in this country? Can it be done quickly and without a fuss? What sort of guarantee do you get with it? Is there plenty of stock available? These days I would avoid systems that are made abroad because you immediately have post and package problems. Customs will charge vast sums occasionally and are excellent at holding things up. You may often have a long wait for repairs. Go to a good reputable

Telemetry equipment. Whatever sort you buy, make sure it has a good after-sales service – and practise with it as much as possible

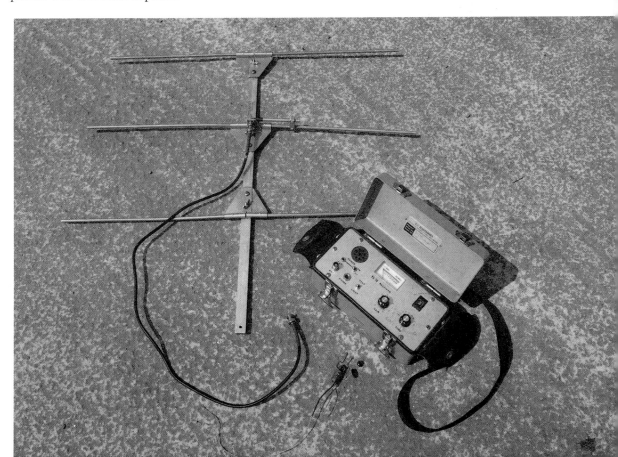

supplier, preferably without a bankruptcy record! If possible meet the actual people who are making or having the equipment made rather than a dealer.

How to Use Telemetry

Once you get a set you should immediately try it out and learn how to use it so that should the worst happen and you lose a bird you are not trying to find it and learning about the equipment at the same time. First of all try it in a field and put the transmitter on a fence and see how you follow the signal. See which way to hold the aerial, how to use your body to shield the signal, how to turn down the signal as you get closer. Then get a friend to hide it a little further away and try again. Then get someone to drive a fair distance away and try again. Another good trick is to get someone to put it on a dog for you. Wrap it around the collar with tape and try tracking that – that's a test I can tell you! If you have problems ask the supplier for help, don't immediately assume the stuff is no good – it could be you!

We have three high points round here where we go if we can't pick up the signal from a lost bird. If we are having no joy picking up a signal we may wait until dark and then go to a high point downwind from where we lost the bird and try to pick up a signal when the bird has stopped moving. It tends only to be the falcons that will go a long way. Hawks, eagles, buzzards and owls will all tend to stay relatively close to where they were lost, at least in the first couple of days. As a last resort if we have lost a bird away from home and are not having any luck, we may find a local airport with a flying club and pay someone to take us up to see if we can get a signal. The best way to do this is to have someone in a car on the ground with a radio phone and ring them or get the airport to ring them if you pick up a bleep, then they can get quickly to the area while you get back to the airport, unless you fancy the quick way down!

I am not an expert with telemetry, any of my staff will tell you that, and I invariably forget to put it on my birds when I am flying them here at the Centre, although I am improving. I have managed to take it down to the flying ground in my bag a couple of times recently! However, when flying birds away from home I do use it regularly.

There is no doubt that telemetry has been of great benefit to falconers and falconry and I would always advise getting a good set if you can afford it. But remember, it will only be useful if you look after it. Change the batteries regularly and learn how to use it well.

Well that's about *all* you will need in the equipment line. Most of it you will need *before* you get your bird. So get saving, get organised and when you make an order, don't forget to print your name and address clearly and give the species and sex of the bird that you are going to get so the equipment can (a) get to you and (b) be the right size. Don't leave it all to the last minute, order your falconry furniture well in advance of getting the bird.

CHAPTER FOUR

COLLECTING THE NEW BIRD

The Collecting/Owl Travelling Box

The same rules apply here whatever your bird, be it owl, falcon, hawk, buzzard or eagle. Anyone who does not have a decent travelling box in stock is a prat in my opinion. A box to transport an untrained, sick, injured or wild bird is different from a box designed to travel trained diurnal birds to and from the hunting or flying field (see Chapter 3). However, this box design is suitable for travelling trained owls. There is bound to be a time in a bird's life when you will need such a box. Why not build yourself a decent one that will last the bird's lifetime and make sure she is safe and secure, giving you peace of mind and credibility with the breeder when you arrive to collect a bird, and with your vet when taking it to see him/her?

Construction

Build, or have built, a lightweight plywood box. The box should be dark, ie no wire doors or windows. A bird will soon settle in a dark box and keep still and calm. Boxes with wire or glass or barred doors or windows will cause a nervous bird to keep trying to get out of the lit area and she may well damage herself. In the case of the very nervous *accipiters* (hawks), the bird may even die of stress. I don't like the American Sky Kennels which are made of plastic with a wire door and wire windows all round. Birds do not feel secure in these and the door and windows have to be covered up, so what is the point of having one anyway, you might just as well get a custom-built box in the first place. The Sky Kennels are expensive, probably more so than the cost of building a good wooden box, and the opening system on the door is dreadful.

An upwards sliding door at one end of the box is the easiest way to put in (or get out) an untrained, wild bird or a sick or injured one. The door can be raised a few inches in a partly lit room and the location of the bird seen. Then with gloved hands the bird can be caught quietly, the door lifted the rest of the way and the bird removed with the minimum of fuss. Side opening doors are much more difficult to work with and we only use them for boxes built for fully trained diurnal birds of prey.

Drill 1in (25mm) holes all along the top edges of the sides to allow air in, but not too much light. Make sure there are no sharp pieces of wood left on the inside after drilling. You can do this before you put the box together and if you clamp an old piece of timber to the plywood before drilling the holes and drill through the ply and into the old piece of 2x1in (50x25mm) you will have a much cleaner hole. Nail or screw a piece of wood, about 1in (25mm) square, running along the outside of each side; it will prevent the box being put really close to a wall and so allow air to get in.

55

The safety catch on a collecting or owl box

A decent collecting box for all types of untrained or sick or injured birds. All falconers and birds-of-prey owners should have one. They also make excellent travelling boxes for trained owls. The floor must be carpeted and note the sliding door

The floor of the box can have a very low perch attached to it but untrained or wild birds travel better on a flat floor. Many will lie down on the journey and the flat floor makes this much more comfortable, particularly if travelling an injured or sick bird. However, the surface of the floor must be covered in a non-slip surface. Rubberised matting; open-weave carpet; Astroturf; coconut door matting: all of these are fine, but they must be clean, disinfected and dry.

Boxes can be stained and varnished as long as they are done at least two weeks before use and then left to air. Varnishing will make the box look smart, last longer and be easier to clean.

Size

Your box should be large enough for the bird to stand comfortably, without stress and without touching the sides or top of the box.

Following are suggested sizes for various species of birds.

SMALL OWLS, SMALL FALCONS, SMALL HAWKS
Width x Length x Height: 12 x 16 x 12in (30 x 40 x 30cm)
BUZZARDS, MEDIUM OWLS, LARGE HAWKS, LARGE FALCONS
Width x Length x Height: 15 x 26 x 18in (37.5 x 45 x 65cm)
LARGE OWLS, SMALL EAGLES
Width x Length x Height: 18 x 36 x 20in (45 x 90 x 50cm)
LARGE EAGLES – ask the breeder.

Air Travel
Note that if you are travelling a bird by air the box has to conform with IATA rules.

These rules change with monotonous regularity. The box that we *used* to be able to travel birds of prey in, which was very similar to the one designed above, was excellent. I have been trying to get IATA to go back to this sort of design, but as yet they still have a very poorly designed box for birds of prey. The latest design, produced in July 92, has not taken enough of our recommendations into account. The person designing them does not, in my opinion, have enough experience in handling birds of prey or owls to do his job properly.

Collection

Always make an appointment to collect a bird, never just turn up. If you do that here you will be sent away with a flea in your ear! If the weather is very hot then organise to travel your new bird in the cool of the day. Hot weather and animals in cars do not mix. Birds, particularly, overheat very quickly and in one case a bird died on a hot day after only 10 miles (16km) of travel. Dogs die in cars every summer because people are so stupid. Leaving a window open is no good, it will still not stop the car from heating up. So avoid the problem and travel the bird in the early morning or evening, still making sure that evening sun does not strike the box in the car.

Once you arrive with your very smart box, on time, if it is a centre open to the public don't expect to be dealt with straightaway. Private breeders will be able to do that and will appreciate you arriving on time, but don't take hordes of other people with you. I don't welcome people who bring four or five others with them to collect the bird and then expect all of them to have a free look round the Centre. I don't mind a couple of people extra but I swear some of them bring a coach! We suggest that if people want to look around, they should do so before we organise the bird and then when they are ready and we have a spare person or moment, we sort them out with their new bird. In this way the bird is not sitting in a box for longer than necessary.

Some people will allow you to see the parent birds, others won't. This is fair enough. Some of my breeding birds are not on view and would be disturbed if they were shown to people too often. But don't panic: after all, seeing young birds in with adults does not necessarily mean you are seeing the parent birds, nor does it mean the young were parent-reared. As long as you have a guarantee with your diurnal bird that it is not likely to be imprinted then seeing the parent birds really doesn't matter. In fact, here at the Centre, the young will probably not be with the parent birds by the time you collect one. They should be in the baby aviaries, learning to be nice adult birds.

Whoever you obtain your bird from will go and get it for you. Under *no* circumstances accept a bird that you have not seen. The breeder/owner should take you and the bird and your nice box into a building/room/shed where you can look at the bird safely and put her into the box without risk of escape.

Check the Bird Over
Check the ring number, if she has one, and most birds require a ring to allow them to be sold. All diurnal birds apart from vultures and Secretary Birds have to be ringed

with either a cable tie or a closed ring, depending on the circumstances. The very occasional bird is not able to be ringed and that will have a UR (Unringed Number). Birds with cable ties and UR numbers have to have a special licence to be sold, although they can be given away without one, which is a bit daft. Only birds with a DoE closed ring and the papers to go with it may be sold without a special licence. Some of the owls also require rings to be sold. Make sure that the ring number corresponds with any paperwork, such as a registration document. Owls don't have to be registered at the time of writing so they don't have a document from the DoE, although it is a good idea to get something in the way of a document from the breeder if you can. This just proves where you obtained the bird, which could be useful at a later date. Have a good look at the bird while the owner holds her before she goes into the box. Don't pay for the bird until you have seen her. Check the following:

- Check that the bird looks well.
- Look at her eyes, are they large and bright?
- Look inside her mouth, is it nice and pink and clean?
- Look at her feet, particularly the underside, they might be grubby but there should be no sores or scabs or signs of bumblefoot or swellings.
- Look at her wings and tail, are the feathers in good condition?

Some breeders will be happy to put jesses and bells on your bird before she is boxed up. *Don't expect them to provide jesses etc for you*, they might be included in the price, but unless stated they won't be. So if you want your bird jessed before taking her away, bring the necessary equipment and tools with you. And if you are bringing Aylmeri jesses for heaven's sake bring spare eyelets as these often buckle or get dropped and I guarantee that you will need a spare when you don't have one. Here at the Centre we are usually pushed for time and are not particularly keen on jessing up birds for other people, not because we are unhelpful, but because we have 180-odd birds and plenty of visitors to cope with and time is at a premium in the summer months.

Once the bird is boxed, make sure you have any relevant paperwork, pay for the bird, get into your car and *get home*, preferably without stopping, except for petrol or the loo!

Fitting Equipment

Jesses and bells will need to be fitted to a new or untrained bird while the bird is cast, that is, being held around the body and wings with both hands. This should be done in a well-lit room, never outside, and with curtains drawn if you are not used to casting a bird. A loose bird will always fly at windows if the curtains are back and they can kill themselves if they hit glass hard. Sparrowhawks and Merlins often do it in the wild in the early autumn. So beware and avoid the problem. You will need two people, one to hold the bird and one to put on the equipment.

Aylmeri Jesses (see illustration pp60-1)
These are pretty basic. The bracelets go round the bird's leg *with the closed ring above the jess not below*. The bracelets are fixed with the eyelet using an eyelet tool. I would

suggest that you do a trial run with an eyelet before casting the bird, then you will know which part of the eyelet goes on which part of the tool. There is a male and female part of both eyelet and tool; the female part of the eyelet goes on the male part of the tool, simple! But try it anyway. The eyelet tool is tightened as far as it will go taking care not to twist the bird's leg, then unwind the eyelet tool and remove it. You should now have one Aylmeri bracelet in place, repeat with the other leg. Now put on the thin hunting straps. You should have a thin piece of leather with a small slot at one end and a point at the other. Put the square slotted end just through the eyelet and pass the pointed end around the eyelet and through the slot. Pull tight and do the same with the other one. You have now got two bracelets on your bird with two hunting straps permanently fixed and all you have to do is put the mews jesses, those with the button at one end and a slot at the other, through the eyelet and put the swivel on the slotted ends.

Swivel

Put the two ends together and thread through the D-shaped part of the swivel, then push the two slots (one on each jess) over the round part of the swivel and pull back up over the D part. Pull right to the top so the leather goes over itself.

Leash

Get the leash ready. The leash goes through the ring part of the swivel. If someone tries to sell you a doglead type of leash with a clip don't use it and don't buy any equipment from him or her. Anyone who thinks that dog leads are suitable for falconry purposes should be shot in my opinion. Equipment for dogs is fine for dogs. Don't put the leash on yet because you are going to put the bells on next. It is always a good idea to put the bells on when you jess the bird because it saves you having to cast the bird again if you are going to put on a tail bell. If by any chance the bird escapes or is lost during training she is more likely to be located with a bell than without.

Leg Bells

When you read this you will think that leg bells are not at all simple – but they are really, I promise! You should have a bewitt strap, which is a piece of leather that goes through the fixing on top of the bell. There should be a hole punched in the leather and after threading the strap through the top of the bell, you thread one end of the leather through the hole and pull tight. This means that when you put the bell on the bird's leg the bell does not touch the leg. You should have another hole punched on one side of the leather as far up as half the diameter of the bird's leg, ie when you hold the leather around the bird's leg with the bell at the back the hole should come at the middle of the front of the leg. There should be a nick in the leather either side of the hole and just above it towards the pointed end. Put the thing around the bird's leg and thread the end without a hole through the hole and pull up fairly tight. Then punch a hole in the piece without a hole as close as you can to the other hole and thread the point of the piece with the nicks through, gently working the leather through until the nicks lock in on the outside of the hole. Then get both ends together and cut them off about ⅛in (3mm) away from the last hole. *Don't forget, the ring must be above the bell if you are putting a bell on that leg.*

AYLMERI

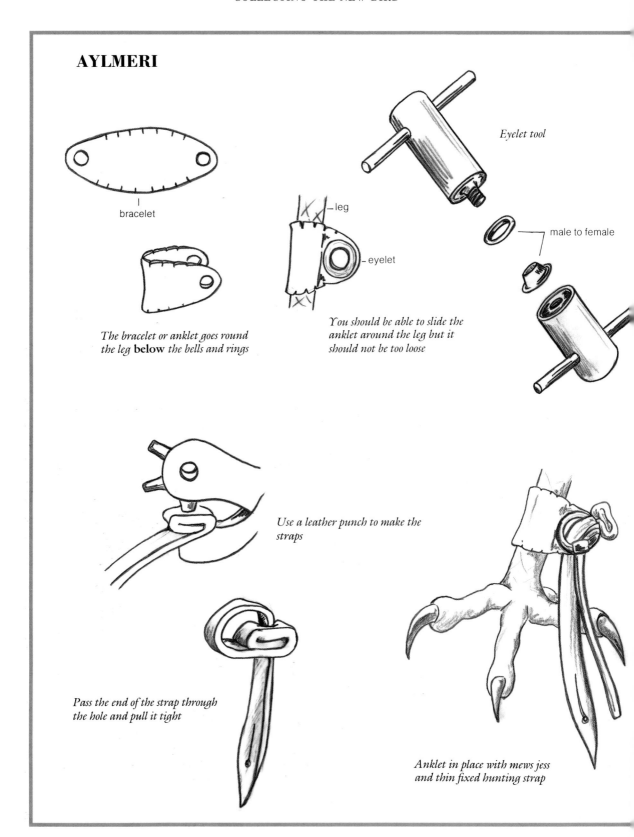

bracelet

The bracelet or anklet goes round
the leg **below** the bells and rings

leg

eyelet

You should be able to slide the
anklet around the leg but it
should not be too loose

Eyelet tool

male to female

Use a leather punch to make the
straps

Pass the end of the strap through
the hole and pull it tight

Anklet in place with mews jess
and thin fixed hunting strap

FALSE AYLMERI *(these are what we now use)*

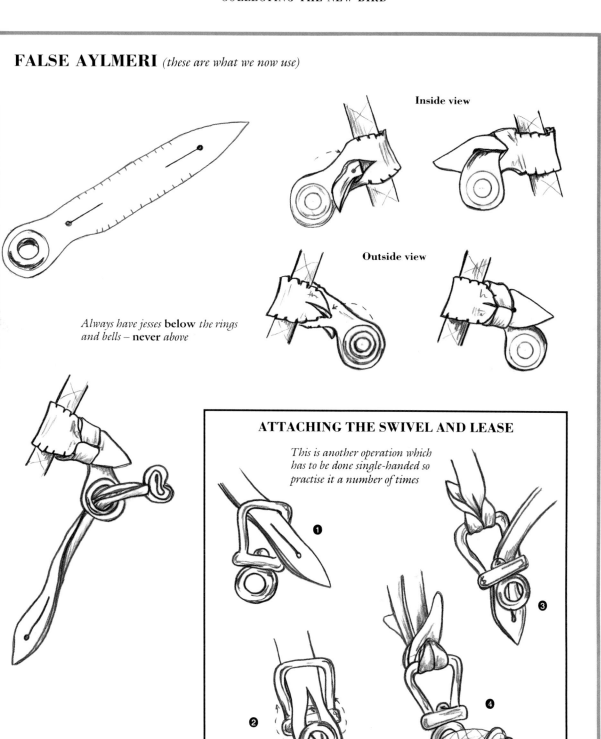

Inside view

Outside view

*Always have jesses **below** the rings and bells – **never** above*

ATTACHING THE SWIVEL AND LEASE

This is another operation which has to be done single-handed so practise it a number of times

❶

❷

❸

❹

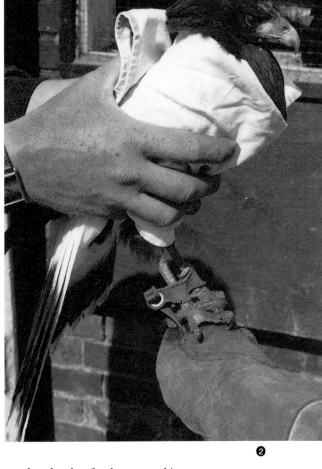

①

②

CASTING AND TAIL BELL

1 *Casting a bird (grabbing hold of her!)*

2 *A cast bird wrapped in a tea towel*

3 *Always hold a cast bird on a cushion or*

towel so that her feet have something to grip. Never leave or hold a bird on her back – she must always be front down or vertical

4 *Putting the tail bell onto a cast hawk*

③

④

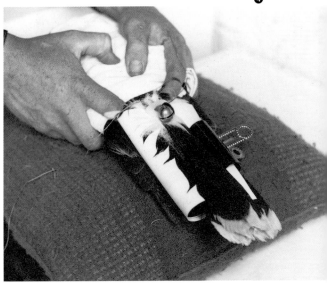

Tail Bell

For this you will need to hold the bird onto a cushion on her front with the tail facing the person who is going to put on the bell. The bird will be easier to hold if you wrap her in a lightweight tea towel and then she won't get too hot. Get the tools ready first and complete all the preparations *before* casting the bird. You will need:

- A piece of paper and a bulldog clip.
- The bell and the leather strap, which must not be greased or waxed leather.
- Rapid Araldite, something to mix it on: a piece of card; something to mix it with: a matchstick.
- Strong cotton suitable for sewing leather.
- Beeswax.
- A curved needle.
- Scissors.
- A guitar plectrum or a flat piece of 'cutable' plastic in the shape of a guitar plectrum.
- Leather punch.

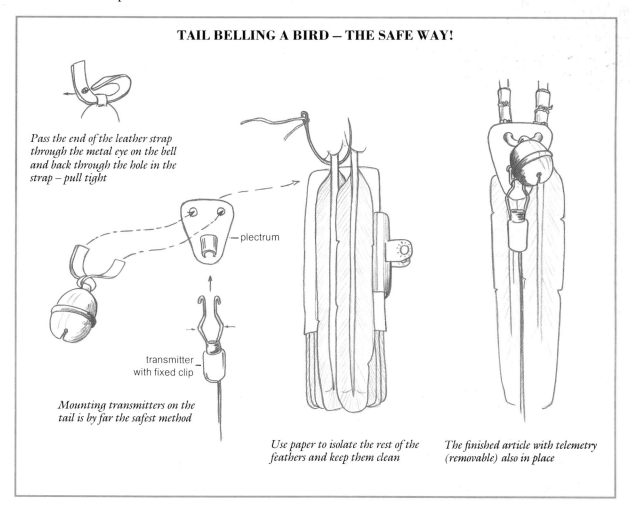

TAIL BELLING A BIRD — THE SAFE WAY!

Pass the end of the leather strap through the metal eye on the bell and back through the hole in the strap — pull tight

— plectrum

transmitter with fixed clip

Mounting transmitters on the tail is by far the safest method

Use paper to isolate the rest of the feathers and keep them clean

The finished article with telemetry (removable) also in place

Put the leather strap through the bell and, having punched a hole in roughly the middle, thread the leather through itself so that only leather touches the bell bewitt strap and nothing else. Punch two holes in the top of the plectrum about ¼in (6mm) apart. Thread each end of the strap through the two holes. You should now have the two straps below the plastic and the bell held nicely above. At this stage if you are going to use a tail-mounted transmitter with your telemetry, you can fix the tail mount below the bell by cutting two slots in the plastic and fixing the tail mount through that on top of the plectrum. Thread the curved needle with about 2ft (60cm) of thread, double it giving you 1ft (30cm) and then wax it with the beeswax. This will make the knot hold while you are tying it.

Cast the bird and get your assistant to place her, tail facing towards you and away from the person holding the bird, feet down onto a cushion. Get your assistant to sit on a chair.

Put the piece of paper around the bird's tail, covering all but the centre two tail feathers. These should lie on top of the paper while the rest of the feathers are wrapped up; hold in place with the bulldog clip. Put the tail bell, now sitting on its plectrum, onto the two centre tail feathers to check for the right length of leather. Cut off what leather you don't need. Mix the glue and put on the underside of one strap, place on the shaft of the feather and then with the curved needle thread the cotton beneath the feather and tie with a reef knot on top. Repeat ¼in (6mm) higher or lower, depending on where the first knot is. Glue the second strap, repeat the two knots. Straighten the covert feathers, remove the paper and straighten and tidy all the feathers. Give the glue a short time to dry, watch the mixing place and you will see when the glue has gone off.

Let the bird sit up quietly and put her on the perch with the leash and swivel etc all in place. You now have a bird jessed, belled, with her swivel and leash on. So leave her in peace for the rest of the day and let her settle.

All this information is relevant to any bird at any time that you are putting on new equipment. However, young birds not yet fully grown, such as owls if they have been hand-reared for flying, should not be jessed and should never be tethered until they are fully developed. Owls can have the Aylmeri bracelets put on when they are starting to run around, but not before. Developing bones can break very easily.

Weight

There is no such thing as an average weight for a bird of prey be it an eagle, owl, falcon, hawk, buzzard, ostrich or whatever. Got it? The same goes whether you are talking about fat, baby weight, half grown, full grown, flying weight or any of the other connotations of that question that I have been asked. If anyone tells you that there is an average weight then he or she is a fool and a dangerous one at that, because average weights can, have and probably will go on killing birds.

Birds vary, weights vary, food values vary, fitness and therefore weight vary, in fact every bloody thing to do with the weight of birds of prey varies! Even when you know the flying weight of your bird, it will vary so please be open minded. Watch, feel, and learn about weights and with luck you will not end up killing a bird by bringing her down too far.

Weighing Machines

The very first piece of equipment you should plan on obtaining is not a glove, but a good weighing machine (see Chapter 3).

Weighing Routine

It is a good idea to weigh any new bird straightaway. It is also very difficult to get one to stand on the scales when she arrives untrained, wild as stink and hating you and every other human around. However, unless she is an eagle, and these are only more difficult because of their size, you can weigh most birds if you have the patience. If things are not going well, make the room dark and the bird should sit still more easily. (Use a torch to see the weights!)

Once you have started to handle and train your bird she should be weighed every day. If you also make it a practice to weigh the food and chart down the weight of the bird, the type and weight of the food, you will learn a great deal over the training period. Remember to feel the body condition of the bird when you weigh her as this will add to your knowledge.

Weight Gain/Loss

Chicken, rabbit and day-old cockerels are white meat and will not put so much weight on a bird as beef, quail or pheasant, for example. So if you are trying to put weight on a bird quickly you should vary the food as much as possible giving plenty of red, dark meat to help with weight gain.

Weight can vary tremendously. A bird can have three different weights all at the same weight. For example, if a bird weighs 2lb (900g), and has done so for several weeks it is a steady weight. If it was 2lb (900g) steady in cold weather and now in hot weather it is not working so well the temperature has come into play. The same bird can be 2lb (900g) on the way up, ie gaining weight so you may well find she is not responding as well as she had done before. Similarly it could be 2lb (900g) on the way down and be starting to go underweight, particularly if the weather changes quickly and goes from warmish to very cold. Then you really have to be careful.

As a bird gets fitter and stronger on the wing and is getting more flying, she will need more food to build muscle and therefore put on weight. If you don't give her more food she will not be able to get fit as she won't have enough energy or muscle. As your trained bird starts to do more flying you will have to increase the weight slowly. This is not a problem because if you put it up too high, you will just find that she doesn't behave very well that day, so bring it down a fraction, experiment and start to put the weight up again a little later. To give you an example, my last female Harris Hawk went down to 1lb 13oz (825g) before responding to training, she was flying free at 1lb 15oz (875g) and by the end of the winter was flying at 2lb 2oz (950g). *This is not an average weight, this is merely an example, don't copy it with a female Harris: experiment yourself.* Two years on she was flying at 2lb 6oz (1050g) on a good day when it was cold. That is a difference of 9oz (225g) over two years and after a great deal of flying and in a very fit bird.

Beginners should avoid training birds in the late autumn, winter or spring. You may be in a frantic hurry to take up falconry, but if you train a nice young bird in the late summer you will have far less worries about her weight and cold weather. If by any chance you get an untrained bird at another time of the year leave her until the weather warms up before starting. It would probably make more sense to leave an older bird to moult anyway and train in late summer.

Public Image

This is a very important topic. A good public image of any animal kept in captivity is vital. It is very unwise, and not particularly kind to a bird, to parade around villages or towns with the bird on the fist (or any other part of your anatomy come to that). Some of you may have seen people doing this, if so, ask yourself why they are doing it! It is unlikely to be doing the bird any good. It does the public image of falconry, bird of prey and owl-keeping far more harm than good. The majority of people who do wander around in public with a bird, for no good reason, are major posers! I am not that keen on people who take their birds into pubs either. It is not possible to house-train birds of prey or owls so the chances are they will defecate everywhere which is not very pleasant for others and again I don't see the point. If you are trying to get a bird tame, she should not be subjected to large numbers of people close by until she is settled with small numbers. If you want to get her tame then invite friends to your house where the bird feels at home, safe and secure and don't risk the keeping of birds of prey and owls by being a prat.

I was doing a flying demonstration at Chatsworth a couple of years ago and there was a man walking around the show ground with an eagle owl on his fist. The owl did not look particularly happy. She was being touched by hordes of people which is very bad for a bird's feathers (as soon as you see someone constantly stroking a bird you are usually looking at someone who is ignorant of a bird's needs). It was quite a hot day and, unlike my birds who had a shelter specially built for them by the show, he had nowhere to put her safely away from the heat, people and dogs. He risked the bird's life by standing close to the arena while I was flying birds, including an eagle, loose, which could, for all he knew, have hated owls. At the same time he risked the sport and my reputation. I had a radio mike so I made sure everyone knew he was nothing to do with me! The point of this story is that birds of prey and owls are not like dogs, they don't feel the same way about their owners and are much happier left safely at home if owners are going out somewhere for the day.

There is a lad in the local town who takes his buzzard through the town. I have had several complaints about him because the bird doesn't like the traffic and so bates or flies off the fist. This looks awful to those who don't understand what is happening and, again, he is doing himself, the bird and the hobby of keeping birds of prey and owls no good at all. There are plenty of places open to the public where people can go and see birds. I strongly advise anyone coming into keeping birds of prey or owls to be relatively quiet about what they do. The more you parade a bird around the more chance you have of someone less than desirable seeing her and possibly trying to steal, injure or release the bird. If you feel the need to have plenty of admirers, then show the bird to your friends at home or join a club. Don't be a 'Robin Hood' falconer or a poser with an owl, you will win no-one's respect.

PART II

TRAINING YOUR BIRD

CHAPTER FIVE

BUZZARDS

Why Choose a Buzzard?

A buzzard is the ideal beginner's bird for anyone who wants to fly diurnal birds of prey. They are a good-sized bird and so will be heavy enough to absorb your mistakes without you killing one by accident. Some species are extremely good hunting birds, others tend to be a little lazy, but all of them, with the exception of the Ferruginous Buzzard, will give a good grounding to the beginner. For people who want to start in falconry, if they are really serious, they should forget the Common Buzzard and go straight to a Red-tail or a Harris Hawk. Although Common Buzzards are good birds, indeed we fly a very nice one here, and I love to watch the wild ones soaring over the house, there is no doubt that the Red-tail and the Harris are better hunting birds. So rather than spending a year learning on a bird that you will then want to replace with a more rapacious species, you might as well spend that time on a bird that will last you fifteen to twenty years.

Common Buzzard

If you are sensible and go on a falconry course before getting your own bird, you will probably have more idea of what sort of commitment you are going to give to the sport and therefore what sort of bird to have. For someone who wants to have a bird just to fly, but not to hunt, there is no doubt that a Common Buzzard is the answer. She will train nicely, learn to follow so you can take her for a walk and is unlikely to catch anything unless you make a considerable effort with her. If

PREVIOUS PAGE
If you want to fly a bird, but not necessarily be successful at hunting, the Common Buzzard is wonderful. A bird happy to fail in catching things, especially with a human 'mug' to feed it. The naturally lazy habits of the Common Buzzard along with small ineffective feet make it a less interesting bird in terms of proper falconry, but a good teacher, friend and companion

you persevere you can get them to soar like wild buzzards which is very exciting.

Red-tailed Buzzard

The Red-tailed Buzzard, which is often called the Red-tailed Hawk particularly by the Americans, is a much underrated bird in the UK. She is, in fact, a true buzzard but unlike our Common Buzzard she has decent-sized feet and is considerably bigger. In fact, if you wanted to concentrate on taking hares then, apart from some of the smaller eagles which are hard to find and expensive to buy, there are few birds better for hares than a good female Red-tail.

Ferruginous Buzzard

The only other true *buteo* you are likely to get at the moment in the UK is a Ferruginous Buzzard. These are birds of the open prairies and unless you have very large tracts of open land, or better still live in or near open moorland countryside, you are wasting your time with one of these birds. They are not a suitable beginner's bird, they are seriously hard to train, tame and handle, the males have feet so small that I have not heard of anyone catching even a rabbit with a male. They are very temperamental and unless you have some experience, have open land and are very patient I would recommend that you do not have a Ferruginous Buzzard.

For a more experienced falconer a female Ferruginous can actually be quite efficient as long as you realise that they don't even hit top speed until about 300yd (300m) into the flight, so unless you have permission over very open hunting land, don't bother. If you have open and, even better, hilly land you can train them to ridge soar, and very spectacular it is too. Don't think that you are going to catch vast quantities though. By the time you have caught up with a Ferruginous on a kill, she will have eaten most of it, so you are pretty much limited to one kill per hunting day. In adult plumage the Ferruginous is very pretty and the dark phase is absolutely beautiful, but before thinking about getting one check that your patience level is good because they are very hard to tame.

Harris Hawk

Last in the group but not least is the Harris Hawk which is not a true hawk, but instead lies between the hawks and the buzzards, probably closer to the buzzards than the hawks. As a hunting bird she is excellent, the added bonus is that she doesn't have the nervous temperament of the *accipiters*. Many trained Harris Hawks do not perform as well as they might because, being so tame, they are often flown overweight and can be a little lackadaisical. However, if got seriously fit and flown on a daily basis, at the right weight, they are pretty matchless birds. I have even heard of people getting rid of them because the bird was too good and caught everything!

So any beginner could choose a Common Buzzard, a Harris or a Red-tail. I would not advise choosing a Ferruginous, even if you did have the right countryside and even if they do tend to be cheaper than either Harrises or Red-tails.

Housing and Feeding

Follow the guidelines set out in Chapter 2. Make the aviary as large as you can without going over the top. Make it as attractive as you can so it is not an eyesore in the garden. Build well, using decent materials, and it will last you twenty to thirty years. Build it so that the bird is comfortable, very well sheltered and has plenty to see and you will have a happy bird for years to come.

The food required by the buzzard family is just as important as any other family group. I do know people who feed *only* their falcons on good quality, varied food such as quail, rats or mice as well as day-old chicks. They then feed all their buzzards and Harris Hawks on just chick. This is just not good enough, particularly as often it's these birds that are doing all the work. You will only get out of your bird what you put in. Feed yourself junk food and you will look pretty seedy so don't do the same thing just because a bird is not a high-powered Peregrine. Rabbits, rats, day-old chicks, pheasant, quail: a mixture will do nicely for your buzzard. A pheasant, feather-on, is only going to cost between £1.00 and £1.50 and that will give you about four days' food supply for a *buteo* – cheaper to feed than a dog!

Finding Your New Bird

To find your bird follow the same rules outlined in Chapter 1. You are unlikely to have physical problems with Common Buzzards or Red-tails, but you will have to be careful with Harrises. Most are fine, but there are one or two lines that appear to have genetic problems. So make sure that you get your young bird vetted as soon as you have got her, if you are not sure of the breeders. A good breeder should give you a short guarantee with the bird and if no guarantee is available then look for another breeder. There are plenty of birds being bred these days and it is very silly to go either for the first one you find, or the cheapest. I always smell a rat when a bird is cheaper than she should be anyway. Price should not be the first consideration when purchasing a bird. If money is such a problem you should not be considering taking on the responsibility of a living creature anyway.

Make sure you have your nice new aviary ready and waiting for your bird several weeks before you collect her. Don't finish the pen in a tearing hurry the day before; this shows lack of planning and will probably mean you have left something unfinished in the rush. Have your weighing room, with all the equipment, ready and a good supply of food in the deep freeze. Select and brief your vet as you are going to get him/her to look at the bird on the first or second day. He/she will start to get to know the bird before you have any problems. Advise him or her of the date you are thinking of getting your bird and check he or she will be around to look at her for you.

Collection

Collect the bird as described in Chapter 4 in the very smart collecting box you have made. Don't forget to check the bird over before putting her in your travelling box. *Never* accept a bird you have not been given the opportunity to examine.

You may have been lucky enough to have had the bird jessed before you get her home. But don't worry if you have not. Check before you go to collect the bird as to whether or not she can be jessed and belled and if not, which will be the usual case, make sure you have someone available to help you when you get home. Also ask what the young bird has been fed on so you will know what she is used to eating.

Training

When to Start

Some people may want to leave their new bird for two to four weeks before training her, and this is a good idea. There could be a number of reasons for this. Some breeders advise this to prevent young birds screaming. Some people may just not have the time to put into a young bird straightaway. Whatever the case, when you arrive home with your new bird you should still get her checked by your vet before releasing her into your pen. You will need to do that on the day you get back or, if you arrive home late, first thing the next morning. The bird can easily stay in the box, placed in a cool quiet place for eighteen hours with no ill-effects. Unless the breeder tells you the bird has been wormed recently, I would advise worming at this stage. We use either Panacur or Ivomec. I have recently heard that Panacur should not be used during the moult. Whatever drugs you use *always* check the dosage with your vet, and ask him or her for the latest information available. Once you have done all this, release the bird and just leave her alone. If by any chance the bird is very nervous and starts to damage herself by flying repeatedly into the wire

Dylan, a male juvenile Red-tailed Buzzard, bred at the Centre. This is an excellent hunting and beginner's bird which is highly underrated in the United Kingdom

Ferruginous Buzzard. This bird is definitely not for the faint-hearted or those lacking patience. They can be seriously temperamental and take real commitment to tame. They need wide open spaces and lots of flying time. However, once fit they are stunning fliers in the right conditions and in adult plumage they are probably the most beautiful of the buzzard family

at the front of the pen, you will need to put something up on the inside of the wire. We use a material made by Netlon, it is one of their windbreak materials. It has hexagonal holes of about ¼in (6mm) with thick black plastic surrounding the holes. Birds can hit it at full tilt and not hurt themselves, it lasts for about ten years in sunlight and is excellent. It will let in light but at the same time give the bird a feeling of more security. This problem normally only arises if you put a new, untrained, bird straight into a new wire-fronted pen. Once the bird is tame this does not happen. Feed the bird through the service passage onto the feed drawer, in this way she will not spend the next month seeing the food arrive from your hand and start to consider you as the provider. This is particularly important with Harris Hawks.

Some breeders are suggesting that you leave your new bird for several months, particularly the Harris again. To a certain point this is OK, but I have a sneaking feeling that none of those who are advocating this have actually tried to train a Harris that has not been touched until January or later! Believe you me, they are no fun, they are wild as stink and very hard to get tame. I sold one of ours that I had kept back to train and then not got around to it. The guy had him about six weeks and then brought him back because he was too wild and difficult!!! We flew him here for a couple of seasons and he got better, but he was never a particularly tame bird, although rather good at catching ducks! I think that breeders are only saying this because they are paranoid about Harrises starting to scream. Leaving the bird until say October is acceptable, but I seriously would not leave one any longer before training.

We train our Harrises in August and usually have no problems. If you leave a bird that you are going to hunt with until really late in the year then you make it much harder for the bird to be entered onto quarry. The bird will be unfit and the quarry will be very fit. In the wild young birds of prey learn to hunt on young quarry and that is the best and most natural way for birds to learn to hunt.

The other difficulty that arises when training your young bird as late as December, January or February is the weather. This is usually the coldest part of the year and bringing a bird's weight down in these conditions is always risky, particularly for a beginner. Unless you have good indoor quarters, it is very risky to have a bird tethered even under shelter because of frosts, especially as a newly tethered bird is liable to sit on the ground overnight rather than on her perch. If you train your bird earlier in the year then by the time the cold and frosts come you will be able to have her loose in her nice pen and the risk of frost-bite is far less.

One word of advice here to anyone who lives in Scotland, particularly the colder regions. Choose a Red-tail Buzzard rather than a Harris if you do not have indoor quarters. Harrises are much more susceptible to extreme cold than Red-tails and more care should be taken with them.

You should get your young bird in September and either train her straightaway or, if you are worried, leave it to mid-October, but no later.

First Steps

When you arrive home, if it is really late, leave the bird in the box until the morning. You don't really want to put her out on her new perch in the dark, it's better to wait until daylight and get the whole process over with fairly quickly. Put the box somewhere coolish and quiet and wait until the morning. You should have organised your time so that you will be around for the next couple of days. Perhaps collect the bird on a Friday evening and have the weekend free to keep an eye on her.

Get all the equipment ready in your weighing room before getting the bird. Have the jesses and Aylmeri tool, the leash, swivel, bells, etc ready. Have the bow perch in place in the sand in your aviary or, better still, on a piece of lawn that is very quiet and away from any disturbance just for the day. But don't bother with a bath as yet.

Cover any window, in whatever room you are going to use, get the box and your assistant and an old cushion and lock the door of the room. Put the box on your table or chest of drawers. In dim light, carefully slide the door up enough to see where the bird is sitting and with your gloved hand get hold of both legs. Once you have them get your helper (called George) to open the door the rest of the way and bring the bird out, holding her away from anything she might hit with her wings. Gently take hold of the wings, close them and hold the bird around the body with one hand, the other holding the legs. Always have a finger between the legs, if you hold them too hard all you will crush is your own finger. George now removes the box and puts it away – tidily. Turn the light on so you can both see what you are doing. George or yourself, whoever is *not* holding the bird, has to put the jesses on, one at a time. Hold the bird with the legs held out so George can get to them, hold them firmly. Put on the jesses, the swivel and the leash. If you are going to put leg bells or a tail bell on, do it now. Don't forget that the ring must be *above* the jesses and the bells, not below. If you are putting on only one leg bell, put it on the leg which does not have a ring. If you are going to put on a tail bell or telemetry mount, or both, change your grip on the bird, place her face and legs down gently onto the cushion and follow the instructions for fitting tail bells in Chapter 4.

Once this is done, quickly put everything away. The bird is still cast in your hands; then, whoever is not holding the bird, put a glove on, take the jesses, wind the leash around the fingers as shown in Chapter 3 and then let the bird go. Hold the bird in the centre of the room so that she cannot hit anything with her wings. The reason you put the bells on at this stage is that it gets all the

TYING UP
It is important to practise tying the falconer's knot long before you get your bird (see page 44).

When tying a bird up, never tie the knot with the bird sitting on the perch. As long as she is on the fist she is under your control.

Complete one knot, then tie a second one above the first.

When returning a bird after training or flying, hold her over the perch to stop her trying to hop down before you are ready

traumatic casting of the bird done in one go, and should the worst happen and you lose the bird before she is fully trained or going loose, at least you have some method of finding her again following the sound of the bell.

Try to weigh the bird. If you gently try to lift her onto your fist, eventually she will sit up, then by pressing the back of the legs gently against the perch of the scales she should step back onto the perch. If you keep the light in the room pretty dim this will help. You need to know what the initial weight of the bird is as a starting point.

When you have achieved this you should take the bird out to her perch. It's a good idea to use a spare bit of lawn where the bird can be safely tethered just for the first day. For the first couple of hours a newly tethered bird will fight the jesses, lie on the floor and generally thrash about, if she

TETHERING UNTRAINED BIRDS

In the early days of training the bird will not sit up while being tethered.

Although this is a Lanner falcon, this method works for all species. Once the knot is complete, place the bird gently on the ground and move away

can get through this stage on grass it is better. Although your sand floor will not hurt a bird on her first day, sometimes the sand can get in her eyes. However, it is not normally a problem. If it is a very hot day do not put her on your lawn, use your pen as that will be cooler and the bird will not get overheated. Leave the bird tethered and well alone for the first day. If you have her outside, on the grass, you will need to move her into the pen by the evening. Pick her up; you will find she won't sit up on the fist, so get someone to move the perch into the aviary and put the bird back down on the perch, not forgetting to tether her, and leave her. If you live in the country don't leave any birds tethered outside in the evening as foxes will strike very early.

That first day you just want the bird to settle. She is very unlikely to feed, but we usually throw in a small piece of food – a chick, or a mouse, depending on what she is used to – by the perch. You will probably find that the food is untouched the next morning. Don't worry.

This is where you may find that we do things differently from others training birds. We do not touch the bird again until she is sitting on her perch happily, flying back to the perch after she

has bated (flown off the fist or perch) and eating the food that we throw in daily. Training birds is a very traumatic experience for the bird, it can be traumatic for the human too! If you collect your bird, box her, travel her, have her vetted, jess and bell her and tether her all in the space of forty-eight hours, that is enough. To try to carry her, get her to feed and all the other things involved in training, you will stress the bird even more. She will not feed on the first day, is unlikely to sit up well and you are really gaining nothing. If, on the other hand, you let her settle, accept her new home, feed on the perch, get used to her new pen, get used to being tethered and seeing strange sights all before you try to pick her up then the training will be much easier, much quicker and will put less strain on the bird. So which do you think is the best method? We do not use this technique for the eagles, see Chapter 8 to find out why!

Feed your new bird every day, first offering the food she is most used to. If you get a bird from us here at The National Birds of Prey Centre, the bird will be used to all types of food, even beef. Other breeders may not feed such a variety so remember to ask this when you collect the bird. If she is only used to eating chicks, use these at first and then introduce rabbit, quail and beef. Throw the bird as much as she will eat. She should feed on the perch by the third or fourth day. Continue until she is flying down onto the food and eating well, about a week to ten days.

Starting Work

We start work when the bird is feeding and sitting up on her perch. Put on your falconry bag and cut a piece of nice tender meat: you can use beef, a rabbit leg or a skinned, gutted quail. Slash the meat so that bits will come away very easily, put it in your bag. Don't feed the bird on the ground that day, go in and pick her up. She will definitely bate away from you so you need to go in quickly, don't run, but don't hang about. Get hold of the leash with your gloved hand, run it up the leash and take the jesses. With your bare hand put the jesses into *safety position* (see overleaf). Hold the bird at the full length of the leash above the perch, so that her wings are not hitting the ground or the perch. Undo the leash, stand up, away from the perch, halve the leash and wind the two ends around the fingers of your bare hand. Take the jesses out of safety position and lay them down

the front of your gloved hand, wind the leash once around the little finger tightly and once around your fourth finger (wedding finger – the one next to the little finger!) with all the ends meeting (see photo on page 76). During all this the bird is probably hanging upside-down so don't take hours about it. Try to get the bird to sit up, you may find that she will get up of her own accord. Don't be surprised if this happens, it is because you gave her time to settle and get to understand about perches and jesses before you started to handle her. Some people feel more confident if they tie the end of the leash to their glove, some even have a short piece of leash permanently fixed to the glove with a clip on the end which they attach to the swivel. Whichever method you use remember that the whole point of having the leash wound neatly around your fingers is to get it out of the way of the bird when she bates off the fist.

Now walk slowly out of the pen through the service passage and slowly into the weighing room. Lock the door, get the bird back on the fist again if she has bated which she almost undoubtedly will have done. You can do this in two ways: either lift her from her front or her back. I find the lift from the back is less painful – to the human – as the bird can't bite you! Now weigh the bird. She will have probably lost weight from the weighing you did on the first day because she will not have fed on the perch for perhaps two or three days. However, don't worry as that is what you want at this stage. If she hasn't lost weight, again don't worry, she will start to do so now.

There are a lot of people advising beginners to bring the weight of new birds down slowly and I have had several phone calls from people who have only been giving their birds small rations for a month to six weeks and they are wondering why the training is not going well. If you seriously want a bird to become a screamer then the *very best way* to do it is to bring the weight down slowly. I really wish some of these people would think logically about what they are doing. Their bird is on the edge of hunger for weeks at a time without her gaining anything. After a while, particularly if she is a Harris Hawk, she will be screaming her head off for food because she is always hungry. Once that starts you will find it very difficult to stop. If it is a Red-tail this is when they start to get footy. The fault lies not with the breeder, as long as he or she has done her job properly, but with the training method.

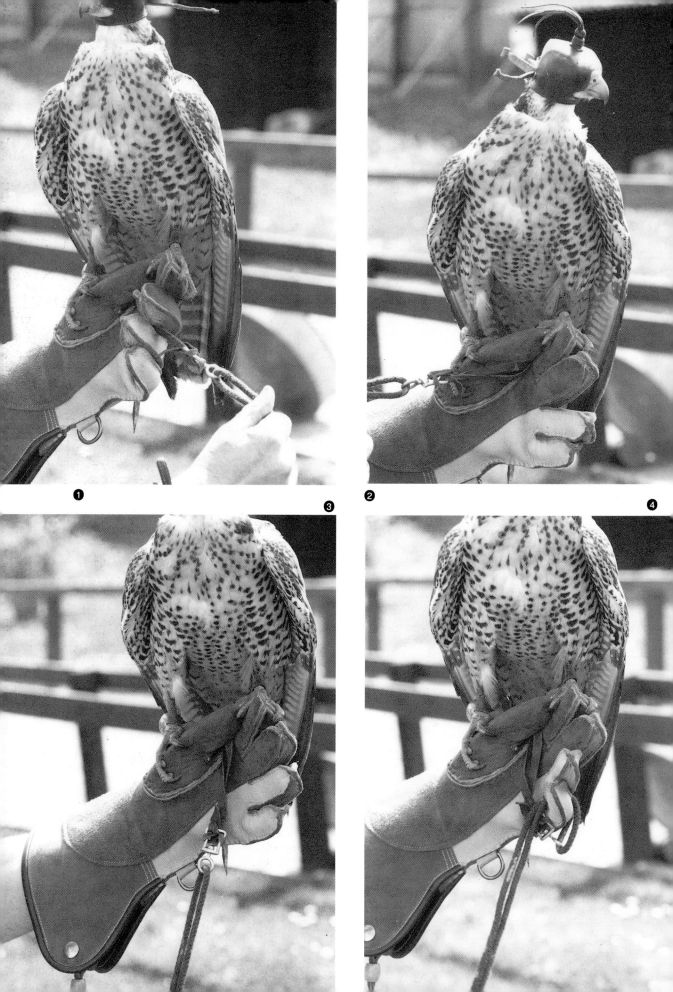

❶

❷

❸

❹

THE SAFETY POSITION

1 Tucking the swivel through the fingers means that the jesses can't slip. The safety position should become as automatic as breathing

2 Take the swivel out of safety and lay it in the centre of your hand

3 You must coil the leash neatly once the bird is on the fist and away from the perch.

4 The leash is wound fairly tightly round the little finger, still leaving the bird jess room to move. Note the D ring. This can be used for tying the leash if beginners feel more secure with this method

5 A neatly coiled leash won't tangle around a bird if she bates

❺

We expect to get a Harris Hawk, Red-tail or Common Buzzard going free in twelve to fourteen days from the first day we pick them up, after they have learnt to feed on the perch before initial handling. In fact we have had at least three Harris Hawks hunting within a fortnight of first picking them up. Our method is to cut the bird down in weight very quickly and as soon as you are getting a result, put the weight up again. This means that the bird is not hungry for weeks, but only a matter of days. This is much better for the bird and means that you get her flying free and hunting all the sooner. That is the method I am going to describe.

Day 1

Weigh the bird and chart the weight. We usually weigh our birds with the leash off but the swivel still on. Lift the bird from the weighing machine and, having gone into safety position first, thread the leash back through the swivel. Come out of safety position, and then put the jesses down the middle of the gloved hand and the leash neatly wound around the fingers. To lift the bird from the scales you will find that if you hold on tightly to the jesses and lift your fist the bird will have to step up. You can do it from the back by pressing the gloved hand against the legs of the bird and she should step back onto the glove. All these movements should be slow but firm. Now move gently out of the weighing room and find somewhere quiet and peaceful to sit with your bird. If the weather is awful you will have to do this in-doors, but it is much better to get the bird to feed outside as it is more difficult and so you will have gained more.

Put the meat into your hand and encourage the bird to feed. Touch her feet and wiggle the meat about in the glove. Don't pick it up and stick it under the bird's beak, this doesn't achieve much. Try for about half an hour and if nothing happens then stop. Put the meat away in your bag and gently get up and take the bird back to her pen and put her back on the perch, tethered. Do not give her any food at all. She is only allowed food at this stage when she feeds from the fist.

During this period the bird will probably have bated off the fist several times, just lift her carefully back up. Do be careful, though, because a grab from something like a female Red-tail is very painful so use the lift from behind. When you replace the bird on the perch, try to keep her on the fist, even if it means it takes five or ten minutes. Hold your fist above the bow perch to avoid her wanting to jump onto the perch before you are ready. Take hold of the leash and unwind it from the fingers of the gloved hand, put the jesses into safety position, pull the leash through the swivel

PICKING UP A WILD BIRD FROM THE PERCH

1 *Picking up a new, untrained Lanner. Note the swivel is in the safety position while the leash is being folded in half*

2 *The bird is still bating while the leash is sorted out*

3 *I leave the bird down until the leash is in position*

RIGHT
These two photographs show the falcon getting up onto the fist by itself

PICKING UP A BIRD THE WRONG WAY

This is the way to pick up a bird if you want to get bitten – and it's downright dangerous with a Red-tail or Golden Eagle (see two photographs below)

PICKING UP A BIRD

1 *The best and safest way to pick up a bating bird. Keep your hand around the lower back*

2 *Move your hand around the body under the wings, and lift the bird*

❶

❷

PICKING UP A TRAINED BIRD FROM THE PERCH

1 *Picking up a bird without using food. Note the low approach to avoid upsetting the bird*

2 *When you have hold of the jesses, lift the hand up gently*

3 *As the hand moves up the bird will step up*

until the knot is hard against the ring of the swivel. Make a habit of doing this because, occasionally, you may be tying a bird up in the dark and if you make it a habit you will not tie the bird up with the wrong end of the leash! Tie your falconer's knot and then open your hand so the jesses are free. Drop the gloved fist gently below the perch and the bird should hop off. If not, try dropping her tail behind the perch and pressing the legs against the perch. Make sure that you are not leaning over the bird or it will be very uncomfortable for you. Kneel or lean away from her and she will be more likely to get off. Then, keeping low, move slowly away from the perch and leave the bird until the next day.

Day 2

Next day do exactly the same thing. Pick the bird up from the bow perch. Again she will bate away so pick her up quickly and into safety position with the jesses. I can't stress enough how safety position should become a way of life to anyone handling trained birds. It should be an automatic reaction that you do every time you pick up a bird or put her down or take off the swivel. You should do it without even thinking. Untie the leash and move away from the perch. Get the leash in the correct position, that is, wound around the fingers if you are like us, or tied to the glove or clipped to the swivel. Go and weigh the bird and chart the weight. You should have some weight loss but it may not be great as the bird will only have been without food for one day so far. Sit down with your nicely slashed piece of meat or rabbit leg or whatever, but not day-old chick. You will have got the bird used to different food types, although you may have to resort to a day-old chick for the first feeding on the fist, but have a piece of beef or rabbit on there at the same time.

PICKING UP A WILD BIRD FROM THE PERCH

1 When picking up a wild bird from the perch, it will bate away, so run your gloved hand up the back quickly

2 Lift the bird up off the ground

3 Hold the bird at leash length well away from the perch, and get the swivel into the safety position

4 Undo the leash and move quickly out into the open

The bird will soon feed on the other food types and you can get rid of the chick.

Give her half to three-quarters of an hour with the food. If you see the bird licking her lips (beak!) then you will know you are getting close. If she does not feed, take the food away and put the bird back on the perch without anything to eat.

Day 3

Try again the following day, pick up, weigh, man and try to feed (see page 84 for explanation of manning). By the third, fourth or fifth day she should feed. I have had a very fat Harris go ten days before she fed and that is pretty scary. Once she does feed give her a full crop, as much as she can eat. Then sit quietly for another half an hour or an hour before putting the bird back on her perch. After you have replaced her on the perch, sit next to the perch for ten minutes or so and just be there, talk to her. Spend some time with her. Move away slowly, and low, and quietly when you leave. You can also put a bath by the perch at this stage as the bird will be taming down enough to think about having a bath or a drink. It will also help should she be getting a little dehydrated. Put the bath to the side of the bow perch, not in front or behind where the droppings will go.

Day 4

The next day you are going to do the same thing, but when you have picked the bird up, instead of untying her and moving away quickly, sit or kneel by the perch. Once the bird is sitting up on the fist, put her back on the perch slowly and try to pick her up with a small piece of meat without her bating. You may have to do this several times before it works, but it is the start of teaching a bird to pick up well. Then go through the usual routine of safety position, untying, weighing, charting the weight and feeding on the fist. She should have gained a little weight, but she may still drop a little or stay level. Feed again as much as possible. Man for a while, perhaps try walking slowly around with the bird on the fist for an hour or so. You can, at this stage, bring her into the house and have her on the fist while watching TV. But remember to put newspaper on the floor and sit in a part of the room where you are away from either people coming in or going out or breakable things that could get hit by wings when the bird bates.

Some people, when their bird is flying free, tend to let her go every time she bates, particularly letting her sit on gate posts or fences. It is a very bad habit as you will find that you have a bird that bates consistently as she is used to being allowed to go when she wants. It also means that the bird will often be in the wrong place just when you have found quarry or has frightened the quarry away because of the noise of the bells. Now is the time in the training to avoid this problem. *Never* let the bird think she will be allowed to sit on gate posts or fences when you walk past them in the manning process. As the bird gets more used to the training you may well find that she bates at suitable perches. We find the best way to cope with this is to raise your gloved hand above head height when you are going to allow the bird to leave the fist, but never let it go when your hand is in the normal carrying position. This means you are giving the bird a signal by raising your fist and she knows (eventually) when she is allowed to fly off and when not. If you can succeed with this training once you have a bird hunting well, when she bates off the fist, theoretically, she will be bating at quarry you have not seen and not just to sit on an inviting perch.

From now on give her as much manning as possible, but leave it until this stage when she has started feeding as then she will feel she is gaining something from you.

Day 5

You are now going to ask the bird to jump to the fist if the weather is good. Don't try doing this on a rainy or a windy day, you need it nice and calm. Find a sheltered spot near a decent post or perch of some sort. Make sure you are well away from trees. If you don't have a suitable post with a top of at least 4in (10cm) diameter, you can make yourself a moveable perch similar to the one I use away from home. It is just a piece of 4 x 2in (10 x 5cm) timber covered in carpet on top of a hinged A-frame. It can be opened out and placed anywhere and then folded up and placed back in a car. The perch or post should be about 4ft (1.2m) high. Do the usual picking up, safety position, leash in the right place, weighing, etc. Then with your bag and an unslashed piece of meat (from now on the meat should be more difficult for the bird to eat from and not very tender) walk the bird to the flying perch. This part of the training can be done in your garden as long as it is a

RETURNING A BIRD TO ITS PERCH

1 Once the knot is tied get the bird back on the fist and then replace her on the perch. The fist is held well below the perch, and the bird moves naturally up to the higher point

2 Drop the hand away gently

3 Keep your body away from the bird

reasonable size, as the bird is only going to jump a short distance to start with.

Give her a little nibble on the fist and then remove the meat. To do this you hold the end of the meat below your gloved thumb and pull it away quickly with the bare hand and put it straight behind your back and then into your bag. If you hesitate or take a long time about this, one day the bird will grab your bare hand holding the meat and you will look very silly. It's a good idea, at this stage, to cut longer than needed pieces of meat, fairly tough stuff such as shin of beef. The length gives you enough to hold onto when you take it away from the bird. A rabbit leg is good too because the foot makes a good handle. Alternatively, instead of using a large piece at this stage, you can cut tiny pieces and put them on the glove. I tend to do this a little later on in the training. Waving around a large piece of meat means you can attract the bird's attention more easily.

Undo the leash from your fingers, holding the two ends very securely, then pull the knot up to the swivel, and tie the other end of the leash to your glove. Don't stand too close to the flying perch or the bird may be trying to bate towards it. Once the leash is tied safely, put the bird on the perch and hold your gloved hand about 6in (15cm) away and slightly higher than the perch. Encourage the bird to look at the meat. Whistle to the bird.

You are looking for a step up to start with and then a small jump to the fist, but the important thing to remember here is that you want a fairly quick result. If you stand there for forty minutes the first time you may well get the bird to jump, eventually, but you will also be well on the way to teaching her to take her time to come. It is far better to get a step up in a couple of minutes than a jump or hop in ten minutes. If the bird is not responding within five minutes, go back to a step up and leave it at that. Don't feed the bird more than a few mouthfuls as we now want her to lose a little weight. Do give her a couple of hours of manning, that is, walking around, sitting and generally carrying the bird to get her tame and used to strange and wonderful things. If the bird does well and jumps a couple of times after the initial step up, give her a good feed and then continue with the manning. Remember to whistle every time you call the bird to the fist, both in the training and off the perch when picking up.

Day 6

The next day do the same things: picking up, weighing, taking her to the training area; then secure the leash onto the glove and see if the bird will jump. She should do it today if she stepped up yesterday. Spend about fifteen minutes on persuading her to jump, but no longer. If she doesn't, then end on a step up to the fist, and leave it at that. Don't feed much food and give as much manning as you can before returning the bird to the perch. If the bird does jump then do no more than four jumps, each a little farther apart. Try to get 4ft (1.2m) away for the last jump, ie a full leash length. The reason for only asking the bird to jump four times is that each time she comes she will have a reward. That takes the edge off her appetite and she will get slower to respond if you continue too long. It's a quick response you want. Once you have achieved the four jumps to the fist, feed the bird and man it for as long as you can manage.

There is no reason why you shouldn't put the bird down on her perch after a training session and then pick her up again later for a manning session. The only thing to remember is that you want to give yourself plenty of time to pick the bird up from the perch. Take in a piece of meat to help with the pick-up. If the bird bates away, just kneel quietly near the perch and wait for the bird to fly back onto it. You may find that by putting a tiny piece of meat on the perch you can encourage her back and then lean forward slowly and offer the glove with the pick-up piece. Once the bird has stepped up, let her settle for a minute before bringing in your bare hand to take the jesses and then carry on as usual, not forgetting *safety position*, which I will bug you about at all times!

Advanced Work

You should practise putting the creance on at home in the house without a bird. Just have your spare swivel and jesses put together and hold them in your gloved hand and try tying the creance on, one-handed; it is not easy to practise it. You tie it on with two normal falconer's knots. Once the creance is in place you can take off the leash, fold it in half and in half again and loop the strap round on your falconry bag, then you won't lose it.

From now on, each day you are just going to ask the bird to come further, which means you are going to use your creance or training line. Take it with you in your bag to the flying area (I am assuming that most of you have a garden big enough to do the initial training, it is a bit hard on the bird if you have to travel with her straight-away before she is trained). Stand at a reasonable distance from your post or mobile perch, or with your back to it, because, by now, the bird will have learned what it is for and will try to get onto the perch if you stand in the wrong place. Thread the end of the creance through the swivel, while the leash is still on it, wound up neatly in place.

When the creance is on safely, take off the leash and put the bird on the perch, then walk away, gently unwinding the creance without pulling the bird off the perch. Put the remainder of the creance still on its stick, because at this stage you do not need to unwind much more than about 10ft (3m), in either your right-hand pocket or your falconry bag. Some people say that you should tie the creance directly to the jesses and remove the swivel, so that should the worst happen and the creance breaks the bird will be less likely to get tangled up. The problem with this is that if the bird goes off at speed and you have to bring her down with the creance, the thin, very strong, nylon line of the creance is more likely to cut through the jesses and indeed I had it happen with a young Lanner in January 1993. Luckily, and it was very, very lucky, she was recovered three weeks later. Another week and she would have been dead. So I stick to tying the creance to the swivel as I have never had a good creance break in thirty years.

Walk back gently to the bird and offer the meat on the glove, making it very obvious. Wave the meat about for a couple of seconds and then slap it onto the glove – whistle. Always start off with a very short jump just to encourage the bird. Then double the distance and if that works, double it again. With large gestures (polite ones) pat your glove to attract attention. If the bird doesn't come readily, go in a little closer. Do this no more than four to six times at the most. If the weather is windy, always call the bird into the wind. Keep gently pushing the weight up and if the bird does not respond as well on one day, then drop her weight fractionally and keep it at that for a while before pushing it up again. The patting of the glove is quite useful because if, at a later date, you want a bird to land on a certain perch you can pat the perch with your hand and the bird will already understand that gesture and have the idea of coming to that area.

PICKING UP A TRAINED BUZZARD

1 *Calling a trained Buzzard to the fist for meat*
2 *Put the jesses into safety before removing the meat*
3 *Safely in safety position*

REPLACING A BUZZARD ON A BOW PERCH

1 To get a bird to go back to its perch, drop your fist below the level of the perch and she will fly back automatically

2 When replacing the bird on the perch hold her well above the perch while tying the knot

After a few more days your bird should be coming pretty readily to the fist the full length of the creance. Occasionally you may find that the bird, finding herself flying sometimes higher than you and your fist, will go straight over the top of the fist. This is when you grab the creance line which is either in your bag or your right-hand pocket. If you are flying a large female Red-tail try to get hold of the line with your gloved hand, because if you have the line run through your bare hand trying to stop a large bird you can get a very nasty nylon rope burn which takes ages to heal. Bring the bird down slowly, not with a jolt, and then, walking around to the front of the bird, see if you can get her to fly up from the ground to your fist. You may have to go in quite close but *do it slowly*. Go back to the perch, try a much shorter jump to the fist and end the session there. Always try to end a training session on a good note even if it means the training goes backwards a little. By this time you must be training your bird in a fairly large open area because the last thing you want a

bird to do, on a creance, is get caught up in a tree. Make sure that your line is shorter than the distance to the nearest available tree.

Flying Area
Once the bird is starting to come well, if you have now outgrown your garden, you should organise a safe place to do your training. What you need is a reasonable sized field with short, grazed grass. If the grass is long it will really hinder the training as the creance will get caught up the whole time and that will seriously upset the bird. If the grass is rather long, or has a lot of thistles and the like, ask the owner if you can mow a strip so that the creance can run freely. Offer to mow down his thistles or nettles if he has them, that will put you in good stead, or hand him or her a bottle of decent wine – bribery works a treat! Ideally the flying area for training should be as close to your home as possible and if you can walk to it without taking the bird through the middle of a town or busy village, better still. However some people

will have to travel by car, in which case you will need your travelling box (see page 45).

Bring in your now taming down, semi-trained bird, lock the door, and gently drop the bird as low as you can so that she is not tempted to sit on the top of the open door. Show her the perch inside the travelling box and see if you can get her to step off onto it, maybe even have a tiny piece of meat on the perch to encourage her. Have the leash fully through the swivel up against the button and hold the other end, or tie it to your glove. Get your pick-up piece, or a small piece of meat, and see if the bird will hop off the perch and onto your fist. If she tries to fly straight out of the box, get her back on the fist and try again. This time, as you get the bird towards the perch and onto it in the semi-darkness, remove your hand and close the door. Give the bird a couple of minutes to settle and then open the door gently. If the bird tries to get out immediately put your hand with the meat through the slightly open door and try to attract her attention. All this takes time and practice, but if you get your bird used to the travelling box it makes life so much simpler. All my Harrises have loved their boxes and have usually flown into them as soon as they have finished and are near the van. I often throw a piece of meat in for them at the end of the day, once they are fully trained, and they dive in after it. Most birds soon feel very secure in their boxes and like to be in there once they know the day is over. For Red-tails and Common Buzzards, make the perch good and secure as, having shorter tails, they don't have quite the balance of the Harrises.

Even if you don't have to travel your new bird in the training period it is a good idea to get her used to, and happy with, a good travelling box so that you can take her out hunting at a later stage.

Many of the procedures described may take you two or three days longer to achieve than I have described. But don't worry about it.

The rules are:

- Don't feed the bird until it feeds on the fist.
- Get short jumps quickly rather than long ones slowly.
- Put the weight up as fast as you can as soon as you have had a response.

Final Preparations

There are a couple of things you need to do before you go for free flying. You should try your bird on different perches in the flying field so that she does not get wedded to the same perch. Remember always to call the bird off into the wind, and to raise your fist to give the bird the signal to go to the perch or gate or whatever. You should also try the bird out of an easily accessible branch. For this you need an assistant. Find a lowish

THE WRONG AND RIGHT WAY TO CALL A BIRD

1 The wrong way to call a bird, with the hand in front of the body

2 The right way, with the hand extended to one side. In this way the space beyond the hand will encourage the bird

1

2

3

❹

CHASING THE DUMMY BUNNY

1 A Buzzard after the dummy rabbit (known as 'Legless'!)
2 Nearly there . . .
3 Gotcha!
4 No, you can't have it back!

branch and have your assistant hold the end of the unwound creance. He must hold it fairly tight once the bird is on the branch to stop the bird from laddering up the tree and getting very tangled. Move away quickly from the tree and immediately call the bird to the fist. Do this a couple of times. At this stage of the training you should have your bare hand in your falconry bag holding the pick-up piece or the titbit ready, so that should your bird follow after you before you have gone very far, you can turn quickly on hearing the bells and immediately have a piece of meat on the fist ready for the bird. Be prepared as they say!

You also need to introduce the bird to the dummy bunny while she is still on a line. (If you do not want to take rabbits, but want to concentrate on feathered quarry, then don't use a bunny but a lure with wings or a dummy pheasant!)

Some birds take to this very quickly, others need to have more time given to them. Bring out your dummy bunny with a good sized piece of meat tied on both sides so that whichever way it rolls it will show meat. Put your bird on her normal perch and do this early in the training session when the bird is at her keenest. Throw the bunny gently on the ground about 10ft (3m) away (into the wind remember) and give it a twitch so the bird is attracted. Several things may happen here:

1   The bird may take one look and fly in the opposite direction. She is less likely to do this if you have fed rabbit and have had your dogs around while training. If she does this you are just going to have more work to get it right. Try having the bird on the fist whilst showing her the rabbit, even let her pull at the meat and then follow the next option.

2   The bird may well totally ignore it. Try pulling the rabbit a little closer but not too close or the angle of descent will be too great. You may have to bring the bird's weight down a little to introduce the rabbit. If you are getting no result that way, leave the rabbit on the ground and call the bird to the fist, then place her on the ground

next to the rabbit and show her the meat. Try to get her to grab the meat on the rabbit and if she does then let her eat it all and settle, then gently lift her off. Do the same thing the next day, but this time give the rabbit a little twitch and see if the bird will grab at it, if not bring the weight down a little and try again the next day. The bird will soon get used to it and start to fly down and grab the bunny.

3   The bird may fly down and land next to it, in which case give it a little twitch and if the bird grabs it let her eat the meat. If she leaps back in horror leave the rabbit still and perhaps go in and show her the meat on the end. You are getting pretty close at this stage.

4   The bird may fly straight at it and sit on it or grab it – lucky you – this is unusual!

When the bird is confident enough to land next to, or on, the static rabbit and eat the meat the next move is to pull the rabbit slowly and increase the speed until eventually the bird is happily chasing it.

By this time your bird should also be starting to follow you, although this is usually easier with Harris Hawks than Buzzards or Red-tails. Walk across the field and if the bird comes after you before you have stopped and put up your fist, turn quickly and put the meat there ready. If she will not let you get away from the post then you may need to put the weight up a little as she could be getting overkeen.

All these training sessions should be relatively short, don't call the bird twenty or thirty times to the fist as she will get bored: a maximum of ten times is fine, plus a couple to the rabbit is great.

Flying Free

It's time to let the bird loose. If you are intending to use telemetry, get the bird used to it before the first day loose. You should know the flying weight (for the bird at this stage of fitness, age, and time of year) by now and you should feel fairly confident. Go for it! The longer you keep a bird on a line the less good you are doing her, it's wonderful to get rid of the creance. Choose a day when you have plenty of time and a friend or two to help. Don't fly too close to dusk and don't fly on a windy day. Go down to the flying field, put the creance on as usual, call the bird to the fist a short distance just to check that all is well, and then take off the creance, the swivel and the mews

jesses, leaving only the permanently fixed hunting straps. Put the jesses and swivel and leash in your pocket or give them to a friend: this is the only time you are allowed to do this, next time you have to do it properly. Put the bird back on the perch and call her further to the fist, then do a normal training session.

When you have finished call the bird in, put the hunting straps in safety position and feed the bird. While she is feeding thread back the mews jesses and put on the swivel and leash, put them all in the right position and go home and congratulate yourself. If anything out of the normal happens – *don't panic* – the bird will feel the difference without the line and may get excited and go up into a tree. Don't worry, she is going to have to learn to do this fairly soon anyway. Let the bird settle in the tree – never call a bird out of a tree straightaway as she will be facing away from you when she lands – wait until she turns around and faces you. Walk to a position where you can see the bird easily and where she has an easy exit from the tree, not with lots of branches in the way. Give her two or three minutes to have a look around and get used to being in a different place and then try calling her to the fist. Don't stand too close to the tree and give the bird a decent amount of room for a shallow angle of descent. Remember, she is as inexperienced as you are and will not have the courage to fly down and land at a steep angle in the early stages, this takes time and practice. If she does not come down, try walking away keeping the bird in sight. Ask your assistant to watch what the bird is doing and see if she is watching you. Unless you have made a big mistake and the bird is well overweight, she will come down. I have never had a bird stay up for long at this stage except for eagles and that is for a different reason. Once she is down, stop there if you are worried or if it was difficult to get her down. If it was easy, do it again! Keep the session short or you might have problems as the bird has more and more titbits and loses the edge on her appetite.

Do this for a couple of days and then try to get her to follow you. Those of you with Red-tails be careful here, you have a bird that can very occasionally be aggressive. If you are going to try to get the bird to go past you and continue flying, rather than land, try to do it between two posts so that there is an easy landing point just past you and keep an eye on the bird at all times. Wear a

Barbour jacket just in case she lands on your arm or shoulder. It should not be a problem but just be careful. Common Buzzards and particularly Harrises may well land on the ground next to you, just keep walking away from the bird and towards a perch or tree that she is used to flying to. Once the bird has done this, call her to the fist and then try again. You can also get to the stage where, once you are confident in a bird, you can cast her off. I never cast, or throw, a bird at quarry – it is much better to let them go if they want to. But it is good to be able to cast them into a tree, try it with your training perch or post first. Face the bird towards the post, hold the jesses and gently throw the bird in the direction you want her to go. Never cast them off downwind, be firm but not rough.

Keep up the work with the dummy bunny. Hide it in different places – get George to pull it for you, make the bird work for it and pull it out at unexpected moments.

Hunting

You should have a trained bird by now, so try to get out hunting as soon as possible. If you are going for rabbits you need to find a place where you know they will be out at certain times. This is where your field and country craft and knowledge is important, if you are not experienced ask someone who is to help you. For a couple of days, before you go hunting, switch the dummy bunny for a dead real one, let the bird feed on it and this will give her more of an idea of the real thing.

Don't expect miracles straightaway, try, try and try again. You may have to bring the weight down a little to start the bird off, but remember every time you have done a weight reduction you must put it back up again. In fact, the weight of the bird should slowly increase over the years as she thickens out and gets muscled up. If you get really desperate, and your bird has caught nothing for months, I would suggest you go to a place like ours which does falconry experience or hunting days and ask for help. Bring your own bird and get them to help you enter it. We have done that occasionally and been successful. But, always remember, throughout the training and flying of your bird you must give her time, you will only get out what you put in.

Living Loose

Your smart aviary has been designed and built to house your bird flying free, not tethered. You will have to decide for yourself when your bird is ready for this. She needs to be very tame and to be very easy to pick up but you should try to get her living loose before the first frosts arrive.

When you think you are ready, take the bird and her perch out of the pen and put her somewhere safe on the lawn. Go into the pen and give it a rake, which incidentally you should do at least three times a week when the bird is tethered. Fill up the built-in bath which the bird will not have been able to reach up until now. Put up the perches and, if you are worried that the bird may hit the mesh to start with, put some Netlon up on the top half of the wire. Because of the design of the pen and you entering from the service passage, the bird will soon learn to be waiting for you near the door and should not go into the wire at the front trying to get to you. Make sure everything is ready and tidy.

Go back and pick up your bird, take her back into the pen, take off the leash, swivel and the mews jesses, just leaving the hunting straps. Pop the bird onto one of the perches and go out, leaving her free. When you next go in to pick up the bird, go into the pen slowly, have a piece of meat and call the bird to the fist as if you were outside. Take hold of the hunting jesses, put on the rest of the clobber and carry on as usual.

CHAPTER SIX
OWLS

Owls are not related to the diurnal (active in daytime) birds of prey which is why you rarely see owls and other birds of prey written about in the same book. They are more closely related to birds called Nightjars than they are to diurnal birds of prey. Writers and scientists tend to separate them because of their different evolution which is a shame really. Owls fill the same niche as the day flying birds of prey only they do it at night. Like the diurnal birds of prey they catch their food with their feet, they are carnivorous, they have powerful beaks and feet. Their young are helpless at birth and they are very attentive parents.

Differences

However, there are differences. Owls have no crop, the food goes straight into their stomach. They utilise their food very differently, the castings of an owl are very different in content to those of diurnal birds of prey given the same food. As far as we know they see in black and white not in colour. Their eyes are very much more vulnerable than most of the diurnal birds of prey and owls seem to close them at the last minute of attack or indeed when taking food from the hand. They also appear to be long-sighted.

Owls rely on sight and sound for hunting and need to see or hear movement, albeit minute movement, to locate food. That is probably why there are no vulture-type owls. Some less experienced people who want to own, or worse still already do own, owls, think that if they have or get an eagle owl, they have, not an owl, but an eagle. Eagle owls, and there are twelve to fourteen different species of eagle owls depending on which you term as sub-species, are nothing to do with eagles, they are not related to them *in any way*. They are just very large, and in some cases not so large, owls. In fact, within the whole group of owls there are only two families: the Barn Owls, called the *Tytonidae*, of which there are ten species, and the *Strigidae*, containing all the rest of the

species, which puts the eagle owls right down to the pygmy owls in the same family! So for anyone who thinks they might have an eagle: hard luck, you're wrong!

We have reared forty-three species of birds of prey and owls here at The National Birds of Prey Centre. We have about sixteen species of owls here now and that should increase over the next couple of years as we are building a new Owl Courtyard. It is easier to make mistakes rearing very young owls than almost any other species. Because the food goes straight into the stomach rather than into a crop first, it is very easy to over-feed them. They also seem to be more prone to upset tummies than many of the diurnal birds of prey. If you are thinking of getting a young bird or of breeding your own owls take care and avoid hand-rearing very young birds; wherever possible, leave it to the breeder.

If you seriously want to keep an owl, the first question you have to ask yourself is why do you want one?

- Do you want to keep her in an aviary, just to look at?
- Do you want to keep her in an aviary and have her tame as a pet, but not fly her loose?
- Do you want to train and fly her just for fun?
- Do you want to train, fly and hunt with an owl?
- Do you want to breed owls?

Some owls are more suited to particular uses than others. The proposed activity of the bird will, therefore, dictate which species of owl you should get. Whatever your reasons for having an owl remember that they live for anything from ten to forty years, which means you have to find someone to care for the bird whenever you are away. You have to have a good food supply and an experienced or willing and open-minded vet. You must also invest in a well-constructed pen to house the bird. If you can't afford to provide any of those requirements you should not be considering getting an owl.

Noise

The one other very important aspect of keeping some birds of prey, and particularly owls, is the noise factor. During the breeding season you can hear our owls here at the Centre *over 1/2 mile (1km) away at night*. What's more they hoot through most of the night and a hand-tame, imprinted, owl will be noisy during the day as well. Tawny Owls not only hoot but have a rape-and-murder scream which they delight on giving at about 3am. It is very loud and quite scary if you are not into owls. Barn owls can make a sort of hissing/churring noise and will do it all night. Eagle owls hoot very loudly. Check on the sort of noise that the owl you would like makes before you get one and please ask someone who is experienced on these matters. Most of the eagle owls will not get their adult voice for a year or more, so don't think you are safe just because a young owl that you know of is not making a noise – it will develop, believe me!

If you have near neighbours you really have to be aware of the noise problem. It is hardly fair to expect them to be kept awake all night by your owl. If you do have difficult neighbours and want an owl, you have only three options: get a species that is relatively quiet, which is difficult; don't have an owl; move house.

Preparation

Before you go ahead with whichever owl you want, first of all, as with all the birds, get your veterinary surgeon organised so that you know he or she will take on your new bird. If they are inexperienced they must be open minded enough to contact specialist vets for advice (see Useful Addresses).

Get your food supply sorted out. Some people will tell you to feed owls on nothing but day-old chicks. This is rubbish, owls need just as good and varied a diet as all the other birds of prey and you will need to be able to get mice and quail for the small owls, as well as the chicks. You will need mice, rats, quail, rabbits and chicks for the medium and large owls. Pheasants and rabbits are also useful as long as they have not been shot with a shotgun.

Build your pen and have it finished before getting your owl. You must have all facilities ready before you get your owl.

What Sort of Owl?

Injured Owls
If you just want an owl to keep in a pen to look at, but not be hand tame or fly for you, then think about having a permanently injured wild owl. The bird will probably never get very tame, you would not be able to handle her but she would be visible in an aviary and you would be providing a good home. There are legal implications to this. The owl must be one of those unfortunate cases that are unable to be rehabilitated to the wild and, unless you have a special licence, the bird must not be on show to the public.

There are many people involved in rehabilitation of injured wild birds of prey that are only too glad to find a good, permanent home for disabled birds. Under no circumstances should you have to pay for one of these birds, it is totally illegal to sell injured or disabled wild birds. If the person offering you the bird demands a donation, or wants to sell you the box they give you with the bird at a ridiculous price, shop them to the Department of the Environment as they should not be doing raptor rehabilitation. *But understand this*, an adult injured wild owl should not be trained or handled, the bird has suffered enough. All you should be interested in doing is providing a smart, comfortable aviary, a good food supply, a quiet home for the rest of her life in return for having the pleasure of an owl in your garden. If you want to train, tame or fly an owl then this is not the road to go down. And anyway, if an injured wild owl is well enough to fly and land, the likelihood is that she is well enough to be released back to the wild.

You will also have to do some homework before getting what you want, nothing comes without a little hard work and effort on your part, both of which may well cost you time and money. Get to know someone who rehabilitates birds of prey and offer to help them. There are always plenty of chores to be done: cleaning of pens or sick quarters; getting food ready and the like. If you like wildlife you should enjoy that sort of work anyway and, at the same time as helping a worthy cause, you will learn. Or perhaps go and do some volunteer work at a *good* bird of prey centre. Once you know the people and, more importantly, they know you are a responsible and caring person, they may well be able to help you with an owl.

Mugwort, one of our Tawny Owls as an adult (above) and a youngster (left). Tawny Owls are very pretty and often good in an aviary, but can be seriously noisy when adult: these are the ones that hold rave parties and can be heard a very long way away at night! Tawnies are great fun to fly, but a little small for beginners. They are also very rarely bred in captivity and so are difficult to obtain legally

But don't expect a free falconry course. The volunteers at the NBPC, and I have some very good and very hard working ones, do not get to handle birds at all until they have been coming regularly for many weeks, doing all the dirty jobs that we do here such as weeding the paths, cleaning the car park, scrubbing all the baths in the aviaries. Once they have proved that they will do this sort of work and not complain, or disappear, then and only then, do they get to do some of what they might call the more interesting work.

OPPOSITE
This female Snowy Owl is a trained bird, and the photo was taken by her owner in the USA. It must be wonderful to fly them in this sort of countryside. Snowy Owls are difficult birds, susceptible to overheating, and should only be handled and flown by experienced people

Tame Owls

If you want a tame owl, but do not want to fly her you can really only do this with a single owl. In fact this goes for any bird that you want to handle. Only birds to be used for breeding can be kept together. If you keep a pair together, they will be interested in each other and not you. If they form a pair bond and start to breed you will become a threat to them and owls will often attack you if you go near their nest. You could keep two males or two females together but again, it is not a good idea. If you want to handle the bird on a daily basis and play with her in her aviary then you will have to be her playmate so keep only one.

Almost any owl that has been captive bred will be suitable, unless you are a beginner, in which case, the old cry: avoid small species. I would suggest that you have one of the less antisocial ones. Barn Owls do not make particularly good aviary birds. If you put up a box for their privacy, and you should do that, unfortunately that is where they will almost always be. They are very unlikely to be sitting about in the aviary in a visible position for most of the time. They prefer to be out of sight and, therefore, are not particu-larly interesting as it were. Of the British owls the most interesting to have, just to watch, are the Snowy Owls and the Tawny Owls. Both are a little more active in the pens and more likely to be seen, which is the whole point of having a bird in the first place. You will notice that I have not suggested that you try to breed from them. There is a glut of some species of owls and I would strongly suggest that you do *not* try to breed from them. You may well find it difficult to find *good* homes for them and I stress the word good here.

The eagle owls are fun to have and are likely to be pretty visible during the day, again this will need some research. You should go and see what these birds look like and how big they are. Find out what is on the market, some are more easily available than others. I am not going to list any as availability is ever-changing. As with any aspect of bird of prey keeping you should do some work, get off your seat and travel to some good centres to observe. But remember that *as beginners you must steer clear of any of the small owls*. Go no smaller than the Abyssinian Eagle Owl (*Bubo africanus cinerascens*) sometimes known as the Dark Eyed African Spotted Eagle Owl. One of

the nicest species with generally a good temperament is the Bengal Eagle Owl. Snowy Owls tend to be about the least pleasant owls to handle, with quite an aggressive temperament. This is a classic example of being able to understand a bird much better if you understand how she lives in the wild. Snowy Owls live above the tree line, they spend most of their time on rocks, tops of cliffs or on the ground. They are relatively clumsy birds and so will not be happy with a lot of branches in their pen. Give them space, rocks, and one or two large perches that are easy to get on and they will be happy. But they are not that good at sitting well on the fist or at landing on the fist. I would say that they are not beginners' birds, but are more suited just to being a pet than to flying.

Suitable Owls for Flying

For those of you who want an owl to fly, but not to hunt, avoid the very large owls such as the European Eagle Owls and the Great Horned Owls and possibly even the Turkmanian/Iranian Eagle Owls. All of these are liable to catch things if you fly them in the wrong place. We don't fly European Eagle Owls here because they catch my hens. For beginners any of the medium-sized owls will be fine, although it would be a shame to fly one of the rarer owls available in the UK rather than letting her breed. We have a rule here: whenever a new species of bird arrives at the Centre we pair her up and try to breed from them first, then if we succeed we allow ourselves to fly the young. Bengal Eagle Owls, African Spotted Eagle Owls, Savigny's Eagle Owls and Magellan Eagle Owls all make very nice flying birds and are a good size for a beginner, being neither too small nor too large. Other species may become available as more are bred in captivity in the future.

Where to Fly Owls

If you live in a town or a built-up area it is not safe to fly an owl loose in your garden. Should she fly away it is almost impossible to follow her over people's gardens. In addition you are liable to get clobbered by an irate householder if you suddenly appear over his garden wall after your bird. To fly your bird safely you must either live out of town and away from the middle of villages and have a *very* large garden, or you will have to get in your car and travel to somewhere away from home to fly on someone else's land, *with permission*. I would suggest that it is not a good idea to fly an owl in a local public park or play area. I used to fly my best falcon in a local park in Surrey for a short time. I had no garden to speak of and this was the nearest place. But with loose dogs around, children racing about, the occasional unpleasant person who didn't like the bird or didn't approve, it was not worth the risk either to the bird or to the image of the sport. So I got permission from a local farmer to fly her in one of his fields, well away from the road. Never fly an owl close to the road: remember that in one year in the UK 5,000 Barn Owls were run over. The very nature of an owl's flight makes her very vulnerable to cars so keep well away from roads.

Hunting with Owls

Hunting with owls is not what most people would call falconry. Very few people have hunted successfully. The owl you choose for hunting will, like the diurnal birds of prey, depend entirely on the habitat you are going to hunt her over and the quarry species you are intending to hunt. Although, without doubt, you could use the small owls and catch voles and mice I would advise against it. Remember that owls tend to swallow their prey whole and by the time you have caught up with a Barn Owl or Short-eared Owl (just to name a couple of examples) they will probably have swallowed the prey and not only be unlikely to hunt again for several hours, but may be quite difficult to get to come back to you afterwards. This is the disadvantage of a bird whose food goes straight into the stomach rather than into a crop, owls feel full up, or more correctly 'fed up', immediately they have fed, particularly the smaller ones.

Most people are going to want to hunt rabbits which would be a natural quarry for the large species of eagle owls. You could take pheasants with a seriously fit owl but I honestly don't know if an eagle owl could overtake a pheasant in full flight. Consequently you are going to tend to take pheasants on the ground, in cover, which is not exactly sport or very interesting. Again this is one of the times when knowing owl habits in the wild helps. There are no specialist bird-catching owls because when owls hunt most other birds are roosting. When they are caught they are usually asleep on a branch or the ground and that is why all birds hate owls and will mob them at the drop of a hat.

Hunting with an owl entails, in the main, taking

rabbits and for that the three types to have are: the European Eagle Owl which is the largest owl in the world; the Iranian or Turkmanian Eagle Owl which is only slightly smaller and is actually a sub-species of the European Eagle Owl; and the Great Horned Owl which is the most rapacious of the large owls, and probably the best for hunting.

Housing and Care of your Owl

Housing owls is pretty easy, the aviary design described in Chapter 2 is suitable for owls. As I have said time and time again, I really don't like open-topped pens, ie those with wire tops. Owls do not particularly like being wet and they do so much better in solid, roofed pens. They also keep cleaner and look much more cheerful. Our basic design will do for any type of owl, ie either for a single injured owl, a tame owl for flying or for breeding pairs. The only difference in the owl pen is that because the bird will never be tethered you need not provide the removable perches as with the diurnal birds of prey. You can make the perching much more fun for your bird. As anyone will see if they visit us here, we don't like perches across the corner of pens. We usually find a good-sized branch or small tree and dig a hole in the floor of the pen and place the branch upright as if it were a growing tree. You have to choose your branch fairly carefully so that there are plenty of perches sticking out horizontally to the ground. If all the branches shoot up vertically then this is no good for the bird to perch on. We get pretty fussy and have some very artistic branches! We also put in stumps, ie short trunks dug into the ground again, the owls like these and will often take their food to them. You can put in what we call our 'budgie perches', large swinging perches suspended from the roof rafters on ropes. However, do not use this type of perch for Snowy Owls and, indeed, give them low, wide branches, stumps and a couple of the largest rocks you can get in the pen as they are not natural tree-perching birds. Have some perches low and some high, this will give interest and variety. If your pen is totally roofed in as I advise, the perches will last you a long time and should not rot. We usually put the perches in just before putting on the wire on the front, it makes life a lot easier.

Owls love to bathe, they also like sunlight, so make the pen just as light as you would for a diurnal bird of prey. As your owl will not be tethered build a fixed bath as suggested in Chapter 2. Our owls love a bath and it works a treat.

Food

Owls, as with any other bird of prey, need a good variety of food. Many people just use day-old chicks but we feel the owls need more than this and wherever possible we feed as varied a diet as we can. If you have difficulty with supplies, find a pet shop that sells snakes or large spiders and they will usually have a supplier for rats or mice. Look up quail breeders under 'Poultry' in the *Yellow Pages*.

We feed our smaller owls on day-old chicks, mice, quail, and grown-on day-olds to five weeks. The quail and grown-ons we cut up into manageable pieces. For example, an ex-layer quail would cut into four pieces whereas a quail at five weeks would probably only have enough weight and meat on it to make two pieces. We usually gut the larger food items but feed the day-old chicks and mice whole.

Small Owls
The tiny owls such as Little Owls I would probably feed 1 piece of quail per bird per day or 1½ day-old chicks per bird per day or 2 mice per bird per day. Occasionally, particularly in very cold weather, we feed a little more. If there is food left over then you are overfeeding, and similarly if there is never any left it is a good idea to up the amounts a little and see if any gets left. If no food remains, either you need to be feeding more, or you need to check that nothing else is taking the food such as rats, Magpies or foxes.

Small to Medium-sized Owls
Tawny Owls, Barn Owls, Abyssinian Eagle Owls, Boobooks etc need the same sort of food in larger quantities: half a quail or 2-3 chicks or 2-3 mice per bird per day. Again, if there is food left over then cut down the amounts, if not then increase them.

Medium-sized Owls
Bengal Eagle Owls and Savigny's Eagles again need the same food in larger quantities but also add rats to the diet. Most of the tiny and smaller owls will not eat rats, in fact many owls don't like

(Left) Jammu, my male Bengal Eagle Owl. I think these are more fun than most of the other owls I have trained. They are the ideal beginners' bird, but, as with all the owls, an owl that has been hand-reared in a group will have a better temperament. As long as the young have plenty of handling by the breeder, the bird will be much more amenable if left with its siblings until four to six weeks old

(Above) Baby European Eagle Owl. A bucket is handy for transport in the early stages – but must not become a habit!

(Below) The Great Horned Owl is common throughout the Americas. They are rapacious birds in the wild and although not as large as the European Eagle Owl, whose counterpart they are in the New World, they make probably the best hunting owl and have been hunted with in the UK and the USA

them, but they will learn to feed on them if you persevere. Cut a large rat in half for the above species and also cut off the tail and gut them, as these parts tend not to be eaten and instead are draped artistically around the aviaries! Give half a rat of ½ a quail, 3-4 chicks or 3-4 mice per bird per day. The same rules apply if food is left or always eaten.

Large Owls

Large Owls such as European Owls, Great Horned Owls, Iranian Eagle Owls and Snowy Owls, just to name a few, can be fed on day-old chicks, quail, grown-ons, mice (although these are very expensive and as a large owl would eat a fair number I would exchange these for rats), rabbit and even pheasant. A whole rat, a whole small quail, a quarter of a rabbit, a chunk of pheasant, or 4-5 chicks should do unless you have a bird with either a smaller or larger appetite than normal. Vitamin supplements should be used no matter how good the diet, see Appendix on page 150.

Remember these are only guidelines for an individual bird and these amounts are not for trained flying birds. These are for birds either not being flown, in the moult or breeding pairs.

Remember to clear away uneaten food very regularly, ie every two or three days or more often in hot weather. (The only exception to this is with breeding birds where the disturbance caused by entering the aviary too often may affect breeding.) Food should be as fresh as possible when fed. Most people are going to be feeding food that has been frozen, but don't keep frozen food too long and make sure it is thawed out properly and in a clean manner. We sometimes warm the food for our birds if we have persistent cold spells. You will probably find that owls will feed more quickly if you feed them in the evening rather than the morning. The exceptions to this are birds that are being flown, or birds that are breeding and may or do have young.

The food ledge described in Chapter 3 is very suitable for owls and keeps the food off the aviary floor which is a good idea.

Don't feed anything that has been run over as you don't know if it was just bad luck that killed the rabbit or whatever, or if it was already ill or shot before getting killed. Don't feed anything

that has been shot with a shotgun. If the animal has been killed by a rifle, check the lead bullet is no longer in the corpse. With any wild food it is a good idea to check it over anyway. There is many a rabbit running around quite happily with lead pellets in it and it takes very few to kill a bird of prey if they are ingested.

Where to Find Your Owl

If you are going to give a home to a wild, disabled owl then we have already discussed what you will probably have to do to find one. You can phone the DoE in Bristol and they have a list of rehabilitators, or the local police may know of someone, as may the local RSPCA.

If you want an owl for a pet, or for flying or breeding, then your only option is to buy one. They vary in price enormously and under no circumstances should price be your only guideline as to what bird you have. If you can't afford over £100 for an owl then you will definitely not be able to afford to build the aviary which is going to cost closer to £700 if done properly. The cheapest owls at the time of writing are, very sadly for them, Barn Owls. However, as I have stressed many times throughout this book, the last book and probably once a week for the last twenty-six years, small birds are not suitable for beginners. Barn Owls do not make particularly good pets. Barn Owls can be flown but again there are owls that are better. Barn Owls should not be bred in captivity, for the time being, as there are far too many of them in captivity right now. They should not be sold willy nilly and unless you have a special licence from the DoE you may not release them to the wild.

The Bengal Eagle Owl is one of the cheaper eagle owls and an excellent beginner's bird both as a non-flying aviary bird and as a bird for flying for pleasure. European, Iranian and Great Horned Owls are all reasonably priced, at the time of writing, and these are the birds that I suggest for use in the hunting field. As soon as you get to some of the less commonly bred, or more exotic, owls the price goes up accordingly.

For those of you who want birds for breeding, find someone who is breeding the species you want and order a pair. Perhaps organise two people so that each knows you are trying to get together an unrelated pair. If you are lucky you may be able to get an unrelated pair from just one breeder. Let the young be fully parent-reared, if possible, or at least if hand-reared, reared in a group with other young owls. Do not get them too young, just before they can fly well is good, then they can go into your new aviary and settle and learn to fly properly in their new home. Don't handle them, just leave them to it and wait until they are old enough to breed themselves. The more you play around with them the less chance you have of getting them to breed.

For the rest of you who want an owl to tame, train, fly or hunt, you need to do some of the hand-rearing yourselves. *But*, and as you can see it's a large but, don't make the mistake of getting the bird too young. Mozart, my now very elderly and very tame European Eagle Owl was taken from his parents (Robert and Shushu) when he was four weeks old. He was pretty antisocial for the first few days, but came to be one of the tamest, nicest owls out. He is now twenty years old, and we still have his father, who now has a younger woman for a wife as Mozart's mother died and Robert is now a new man!

It is fine to have a bird that has had a few weeks parent-rearing, in fact it's good, because the bird will breed more easily in the future if you ever feel inclined. Some breeders, however, prefer to hand rear all the young, leaving none with the parents. I must say I like my parent birds to have one young to bring up as it seems unfair not to allow them to breed and rear naturally.

Hand-reared birds are a little easier than the four-week old, parent-reared birds, but are slightly less likely to breed naturally in the long term. However, if young owls are reared in groups they do seem to breed naturally. The only ones that have not bred have been owls that have had to be reared totally alone from about two weeks old, so they have had no contact with their own species and are convinced that they are humans. Avoid having one of these, they are the ones most likely to become aggressive in later life when they reach maturity and come into breeding condition. Go for either a four-week-old, parent-reared bird and get her tame quickly or go for a four- to eight-week-old hand-reared owl. Some breeders suggest taking a bird at two weeks. *I strongly advise against this*. Unless you are very experienced, rearing owls can be quite tricky. Once they are four weeks old they are past most of the danger points, they shouldn't need any heat, other than a warm dry room at night, they will

Mozart, a European Eagle owl. You must be prepared for a long-term commitment to an owl. Mozart is 22, and I still have his Dad!

Baby owl playing with the gloved hand. Support is vital at this stage

This is Curly, one of two male Savigny's Eagle Owls at the Centre. Sadly, because all the birds originate from one pair kept at London Zoo many years ago, inbreeding has caused the captive population to decline in the UK. Those few females left are very poor breeders, and as far as I know none have been bred for several years. This is a great shame as this has always been one of my favourite owls, and they are very beautiful

be on three feeds per day and will have got to a manageable size. At two weeks they need more heat, more time, they are very easy to kill by over-feeding and they are still quite fragile. No responsible breeder should let you have an owl at under four weeks.

There is also another reason: if your bird is reared with others, by hand, you will still have a nice tame bird, but you will also have one that will pair up and breed in the future should there be a need. I think it is wrong to produce birds that are

unlikely to breed naturally unless there is a very good reason. We don't let our young eagle owls go until they are about eight weeks old. I also believe that the owls will be less aggressive in later life if they are left with siblings for as long as possible. I had a lady phone up the other day wanting an owl she had ordered at only two weeks old and she was quite put out when I would not agree. Think of the bird's welfare rather than your own selfishness in wanting to hand rear a baby.

Collecting Your New Owl

Time to get the owl. Bengal Eagle Owls breed fairly early in the year and there can be young available from December onwards. Iranian and Turkmanian can also breed early. My European Eagle Owls lay in March and hatch the young in April, other people's lay earlier. My Great Horned Owls also breed in March. Snowy Owls breed as late as June, so as you can see, the time when young owls are available is very variable. If you are going to get a young owl in December through to about March you will have to wait until she is a little older before putting her out into her pen. Try it on warm days and if she looks miserable and cold bring her in again. But don't make the mistake of keeping the house too warm. Firstly, if she is too warm she will be more likely to go off her food and even get tummy infections. Secondly, she will feel the cold more when you take her outside. By the time the bird is starting to fly, she should be spending most of the time in the pen, not in your house, but when she first arrives keep her inside for most of the time. From April onwards you can put the owl outside at a much earlier stage which is nice for the bird. Be sensible – take the weather conditions into account and use your common sense as to when the bird should be out and when in.

When you travel to the breeder's establishment take your very smart box that you built for collecting your bird with you, not a cardboard crisp box

OPPOSITE
The Magellan's Eagle Owl (as it is known in the UK) is a subspecies of the Great Horned Owl. It comes from the southernmost part of South America. It has very large and powerful feet in comparison to similar sized African Eagle Owls and is a good size for the beginner, being neither too large nor too small

(people who arrive with crisp boxes here are sent away to get something better). You will have nice carpet on the floor of the box so the young bird will not slip. If you are lucky you will be able to see the parent birds. If you are having a hand-reared bird the breeder may have a baby aviary, as we do, and you can see the young bird in there. If the bird is parent-reared to that date then probably the breeder will have got the young bird out already, so he or she will hand to you a snapping, hissing ball of fluff, with yellow or orange eyes if it is an eagle owl. If she is a hand-reared owl she may still hiss at you as you are a stranger.

Check the young bird over as you would any bird: look at the underside of the feet for sores; check the leg and wing bones are nice and straight; check the eyes and the inside of the beak look healthy; see that the feather growth looks even and if there are any other young of the same species around, check yours is of a similar size. A four-week-old owlet can stand, walk and even do the odd jump so you can check the legs by putting her on the ground to make sure she is standing well. Some people may consider that at four weeks old a Barn Owl is nearly full grown. It is not, owls take far longer to grow up than diurnal birds of prey of a similar size, and anyway as a beginner, who is sensible, you are not going to have a small owl such as a Barn Owl.

You will probably be horrified with a parent-reared bird as she will look anything but tame. Put her in a box, get the necessary paperwork and pay for your bird, check what she is used to eating and then leave, in the cool of the day, and drive straight home with no stopping (apart from the loo). While driving home you will probably wonder what the hell you have taken on. Don't worry, a week from that day you will have a tame owl. If your young owl is totally hand-reared you will not have the same problems but the young bird may well be upset by travelling.

Get the owlet home and take her into the house. At this point if you have an expensive carpet, you should cover it with an old one for the next three or four weeks because, boy, can owls shit!

Rearing

If you have dogs then introduce them slowly to the bird, don't let them all crowd up at once and if you have a terrier or a dog which you are not sure

of, watch it. A quick sharp slap on the nose of the dog if it should show any signs of being aggressive should do the trick. Some dogs are just not safe to have around small things, in which case you will have to let the owl and dog get to know one another through the wire of the pen. It is a rare dog that will rush up to a full-grown eagle owl.

Your new bird, if parent-reared, (please don't call it Wol, Olly, Bubo or any of the other even more unoriginal names I have heard – choose something nice) will now back away from you, she will clop her beak and hiss and generally be about as horrified by you as you are of her. She is very unlikely to feed the first day, but don't worry. Don't leave food with her, she must only feed from your hand, so until she does – no food! If she is hand-reared she may feed straightaway, but don't worry if she doesn't. The travelling and the move may make her a little too nervous to feed. Don't worry, she will tell you when she is hungry by calling for food.

Owls feed by touch, so, giving her the type of food that she is normally used to, touch the side of the beak where there are some stiff bristle-like hairs. If the bird takes the food then you are getting somewhere. If not don't worry, after forty-eight hours she should be hungry enough to get over the initial fear and feed from your hand. If she closes her eyes and turns her head on one side after taking a piece of meat, don't panic, this just means she is pushing the food down her throat to her stomach. Don't spend hours mauling the young bird, but do get on her level on the floor and talk to her, maybe push around a ball made of newspaper as a toy. Stroke her occasionally, play with her beak and feet and give her time. If you stroke a bird constantly you will quickly ruin the waterproofing on the feathers. None of my owls really appreciate being stroked, they will tolerate it, but unlike parrots or Caracaras I am convinced they don't particularly enjoy being stroked, certainly none of them come up to the wire and ask to be stroked like our hand-reared Caracaras always have done. So keep the stroking down to a minimum and your bird will have much better plumage. Slowly she will get used to you. Have an old cardboard box, with carpet or torn-up newspaper, on its side and the owl can go in there as a retreat. Don't put her on a slippery floor or she could get splayed legs or injuries, and a concrete floor is very cold and uninviting for a young owl.

PICKING UP A BABY OWL
1 How to pick up a baby owl: place both hands gently but firmly around the body and legs

2 Lift the owl slowly, allowing the legs to dangle

When carrying the young bird use both hands and, either take the bird firmly around both wings with fingers round the outside of the legs but leaving the legs to dangle, or put one hand between the legs and one on top of the body. Either way if you are firm and confident with your movements, but not rough, the bird will be quite happy being carried this way until she is older, then you will change the method.

Young owls will be more active during the evening which is ideal for most people as this is often the time they have free to give to the bird.

The more used to you, and your family and dogs, the bird gets, the better. However, all young things need to rest as well so during the day put the owlet out into the new pen unless the weather is very cold. This is where your totally roofed pen comes in handy, the young bird cannot get wet, and wet weather can kill young birds, particularly young owls who can get very wet indeed with that thick down coat. If you divide the time for the bird so that she spends time with you and time in what will be her home then she should settle quickly. For those of you getting a young owl

FEEDING BABY OWLS
1 Touch the side of the owl's beak to get her to feed

2 Baby owls will and should eat whole food at a fairly early age

early in the year, when the weather is cold, don't put her out for long periods until she is starting to feather up well, just a few minutes each day to get her used to what will eventually be her new home. Toys are a good thing: a tennis ball is good as it is furry but too large to be swallowed, or perhaps a toy rat; all of these sorts of things make it fun for the young owl.

Feeding

Feed the young bird three times a day. By feeling the tummy between the legs you will be able to tell if she is full or not. If the stomach is hard then the bird should not be fed until it is soft and flaccid. At four weeks old the young bird can be fed whole food, cut up. That is day-old chicks, mice, rats, quail and the like, all unskinned, but cut up into pieces about 1in (2.5cm) across. This size should be easily swallowed by the young owl. Feed until she does not want any more and then don't feed again until the tummy feels empty.

Every now and again an owl will produce a very brown, and very smelly, dropping. Don't worry, this is fairly normal but the rest of the droppings should be brown, black and white. If all the droppings are very brown and smelly then you could have a bird with an upset tummy, in which case you need to give her something to settle it and cut down the food a little. We use a powder called Forgastrin, which is very good, but check with your vet, he or she may know of something better. However, don't let him or her give you something to put in drinking water, it's a common mistake that less informed vets make. This way of giving drugs is for poultry who will take drugs from drinking water – this does not work with birds of prey as they do not drink the amount of water that seed-eaters consume, they get the majority of the fluid they need from the meat they eat. (A tip here, when baby owls are about to defecate they walk backwards, if you are quick you can position newspaper in the strategic place and save your carpet!)

There will now be a period of growth for your owl where, apart from playing with her, feeding her, taking her outside, bringing her inside and generally giving her time, there is not much else you can do. Once the young owl starts to fly or jumps up onto low posts and branches with confidence, rather than a scramble, then you can start on a little training.

Training

By now both the totally hand-reared owl and the one that was reared for the first four weeks by parents will be very tame, and feeding readily from your hands. Indeed you can afford to leave food with the young bird occasionally as this will make her a little more independent. You will also find that you are on two feeds per day rather than three and possibly even only one. Don't worry if the bird is taking less food, the growth slows down and so does the food consumption. As long as the bird is leaving a little food then you are not underfeeding.

I have made a video on owls which shows how you handle and train them as it is surprisingly difficult to describe the whole process in words.

Aylmeri Bracelets

The next stage is to get the Aylmeri bracelets on your bird. By the time she is starting to fly her leg bones will be just about full size. Although there is still body and feather growth to continue for a while, you can jess *but never tether* any bird at this age. You may need to have two people to do this job. You should use Aylmeri jesses with the bracelets, the mews jesses and thin permanent hunting jesses. You will also need an Aylmeri kit to fix the eyelets in position (see Chapter 3).

You may find that you can put the bracelets around the young owl's leg without restraining her. Have someone hold the bird while you put on the bracelets and the permanent hunting straps. It is quickly done and the bird can be released immediately. I would suggest doing this in the bird's own pen and then the trauma is less. I practise using the tool on an eyelet before you start on the real thing, then you will feel a little more confident and get the job done quicker. Once they are on, leave the bird to settle for a couple of hours before doing any of your normal feeding or playing. By that time she will have forgotten the experience. Now you have the means to be able to hold on to your bird but be very careful. Birds have softish bones at this stage, and if you try to tether or restrain a young bird too early you will break her leg and the fault will be yours for going ahead too early. Don't rush and you will not harm your bird. Try to hurry things up and you may well injure your bird, possibly permanently, and definitely enough to land yourself with a large vet's bill.

Training your young owl in the aviary. The training can be half done inside before going into the open

You should not cut the the food down with a young owl until she is full grown. Training is done by means of play really. By now your owl will probably be on a perch when you go into the pen, rather than on the ground. Go up to her at feeding time and get the young owl to lean forward to get the piece of meat. By this time you can also start to get the young bird to sit on your fist. Wear your glove, partly because you will then avoid getting scratched and partly because it is much more comfortable for the owl. Trying to grip on human skin is very hard for a bird. You do get the occasional macho man who doesn't use a glove but we always consider those sort of people to be very stupid and somewhat of a joke. They obviously haven't thought about the comfort of their bird.

Training to the Fist

To get a bird to step up onto the fist, place the gloved hand behind the legs, gently lifting the tail over the back of the glove to avoid damaging it, and press the front of the glove, ie with your thumb against the legs of the bird until she steps back, and then very slowly and gently lift. If you move quickly you will unbalance the bird and she will feel insecure on the fist and jump off again. Make sure you keep your fist a little higher than the perch, perhaps even over it so the owl is not encouraged to jump off immediately, and just keep very still. After a few minutes drop your fist slowly below the perch and the owl will probably step or jump off. Persevere with this from now on, without overdoing it and upsetting or boring the bird. Once the bird is confident with the fist she will be more likely to jump to it.

When the owl is readily leaning forward to take the food, either off the glove or out of your bare hand held over the glove, move just out of reach and see if you can persuade her to take that first jump to your fist. This may not happen straight-away and don't try it after the bird has eaten a fair amount. Do it at the beginning of the feed, then she will be more interested. Whistle to her each time you ask your owl to jump to the fist. Owls use their hearing a great deal and you need some method to get their concentration and get them to look at you, so by whistling each time you give her a piece of food on the fist the penny will soon drop. Patting your gloved fist with your bare hand will also get the bird to concentrate.

Once the bird has jumped, and you may have to cut out one feed to persuade her to do so, ask her to do it a couple more times, but don't go on and on. Always whistle to the bird each time you ask her to jump, remembering that owls use their ears to locate food as much as their eyes and you want the owl to turn towards you every time you whistle. Three or four jumps per day is fine at this stage. If you go on too long the bird will be full of food and less likely to come and probably take longer each time. It is always better to have a short flight quickly rather than a longer flight after several minutes. The length of the jumps can be slowly increased but don't rush things. Re-member, your owl is not full grown yet and you don't want to push things. Jumping to the fist, carrying round the aviary, that is all you need to do until she is pretty near full grown.

Entering the Travelling Box

If you are going to have to travel with your owl to fly her, it is a good idea to get her used to the travelling box early on. Once your owl is sitting on the fist, and coming to the fist for meat, you can try placing her in the box with the front open. Try putting a piece of meat inside and see if she will walk into the box of her own accord. You can even leave the box minus its sliding door in the pen so that the bird can explore and get used to it. We find that most of our owls will actually fly into their travelling box as they like it and feel secure. The box we travel trained owls in has an upwards sliding door rather than a side-hinged one like the travelling box for trained diurnal birds of prey, for owls it seems to work better. You can have a perch in the box for the smaller owls, but the larger ones travel better on a flat, carpet-covered floor. Plenty of air holes in the side and a handle on top make it even nicer.

Outside the Pen

Once your owl has grown to full size you can start to carry her around on the fist outside the pen. To do this you need to have a good hold on the bird, so put the mews jesses through the eyelet on the Aylmeri bracelets, put on the swivel and leash and either by tying the leash to the glove or winding it around your fingers (see Chapter 3) you are now safe and secure and can go out of the pen. Walk slowly to start with and give the owl the chance to see new things. If she should bate, or fly off the fist, lift her gently back and carry on. This is the time when you start weighing the bird. You can do this before now, by taking the scales into the aviary, but it is not really necessary as you will not have been cutting the bird's weight down at all, just getting her to jump because she wants to.

Weighing

Take your bird to your weighing/store/falconry room. Weigh her and chart down the weight, either in a book, on a wall chart, or on a black-board. Do this before you feed her for the day. Then on returning to the aviary, try flying her to the fist in her pen. If there is reluctance to come, or refusal, or slow reactions, don't feed her that day. When you weigh her before feeding the fol-lowing day, she should have lost a little weight and if the result is that the bird is working better that day, then feed her enough to keep her at that weight for now.

Flying

Once the bird is coming readily in the pen, can be carried outside the pen without becoming upset and is at what you consider to be a good weight, try flying her outside. You will need your creance or training line, a clear, open, flat area with no trees close by and fairly short grass. If the grass is long the creance will catch and upset the bird. You will also need a post or perch of some sort for the owl. If I am flying birds away from home I have a mobile perch. It is a carpet-covered piece of wood 4 x 2in (10 x 5cm), with legs that open out on hinges and it stands on its own like an upside-down V. It can be folded away and is reasonably easy to carry. The flying perch or post should be about 4ft (1.2m) high.

With the mews jesses, swivel and leash still in place, tie the creance through the swivel and then remove the leash, fold it up and thread it through itself on the strap of your bag. Place your owl on your perch or post with the creance in place and slowly walk away, unwinding the creance without pulling the owl off the perch. Put the end of the creance in your falconry bag or your pocket, so that should the bird take off you can grab it quickly and not have the bird either hit the end of the creance hard or have her go off near trees and get tangled. Then slowly return to the perched owl and offer her a little piece of her favourite food. You will find that on the first few days of training, out of the pen, the owl will be fascinated with what is going on around her and will have very little concentration. This is normal, you may have to bring the weight down a little to get over this, but once she is responding put the weight back up again.

Always keep pushing the weight up every few weeks, because if you don't the bird will be unable to get fit. She will need the food to turn into muscle. The worst that can happen when you get your owl overweight is that she will either take a long time to come to the fist or will sulk in a tree for a few hours. Slowly you will find that your bird's weight will increase as she does more flying and understands what her job is.

Feeding on the Fist

We fly all our owls to small pieces of beef with vitamins, it is a useful food as the additives cannot get stuck to fur or feather. I do not like feeding chicks on the glove, we feed rabbit leg or half a quail because that is fairly unrecognisable but day-old chicks tend to upset the public and I see no point in doing that. We find that small pieces of whatever you are feeding work well with the owls but small pieces of chick are quite disgusting and quickly ruin your glove and bag. If you don't clean out your bag on a daily basis, the mess left by chopped chick will soon rot, cause infection and smell! Another reason is that occasionally one of our owls misbehaves and either sits in a tree or moves off away from the flying ground. We then offer a couple of chicks tied securely to a creance because most of the birds love this food. Because we don't normally use them on demonstration work the bird will often come back for chicks when they won't come for the normal food used. If you have no fall-back, like this, you are less likely to persuade an awkward owl to come home. As all our birds are given food in the evenings after we have closed, this is the time when the flying birds get either chicks or mouse if that is the food of the day. Chopped rabbit, mouse, rat or quail would work as well as long as you gut them all first. Save chicks for feeding away from other people and for fall-back food with temperamental birds on temperamental days.

Recently someone was fined a sum of money because his hawk grabbed a yellow bobble on a child's hat. If this bird had not been used to being fed on chicks quite so much this would probably not have happened. Take my advice, and years of experience and some of the healthiest-looking birds around, and don't feed chicks on the fist or use them for flying your bird; only feed them at the end of the day in the pen.

First Lessons

Back to the flying field – your bird is sitting looking around ignoring you. Go back to basics, she won't do in the field what she did in the aviary in her own surroundings with little to distract her. Give her time, just go for a step up onto the fist first, then perhaps a hop. If you are finding that she will not come any further that day, then stop there and take the bird home. If you spend hours trying to get the owl to come to the fist on the first day or two you will give her bad habits. You need a quick reaction over a short distance, so if you get a 2ft (0.5m) hop two or three times be pleased with that and stop there. We rarely call any bird in training to the fist more than four or five times. By that time she will have had a fair amount to eat and will have lost the edge on her appetite and be slower to respond. The next day, after weighing, which you will do every day before flying a bird without fail, try again. Always start with a short jump in the early stages of training as this inspires a bird with confidence and reminds her what you want. Then increase the distance by doubling it. If the bird does not come to the fist quickly then walk towards her and ask for a little less. You will soon get the idea and so will the owl. The creance will still be in use as you are a little way from letting the bird loose. If the response is still slow, stop there and return the owl to her pen with no food. By the next day you should start to get a better response and you just continue in this way on a daily basis.

Pick up the bird each day at flying time. Jess and put the leash on before leaving the aviary. Go and weigh her, remembering to close and lock the weighing-room door. Chart down the weight. Either walk or drive to your flying ground.

Creance on; bird on perch; unwind creance and place stick with end of the creance tied to it in pocket; call bird to the fist. This is the routine until the bird is coming readily the length of the line. This should not take more than two weeks. If you have a dog take him/her with you during the training period and it is probably a good idea to have people with you as well. Not only will the owl get used to them but you will have help, and encouragement, available if you need it.

It is a good idea to try your new owl from different perches at this stage. You don't want the bird to be so used to only one perch that she gets upset at a change. Find another post or try the large post at the side of a field gate. Make sure you are not too close to any trees if the bird tries to fly off, otherwise she may get tangled up. We also like to try all of our birds, except the falcons, out of a tree before letting them fly free. We usually find a tree with a low and twig-free branch; at this point have someone else hold the end of the creance. Sometimes a bird will try to ladder up through the tree and you need to stop her moving upwards through the branches with the creance or she could get badly tangled. Just hold the end of the creance tight enough so that you are not pulling the owl off the branch, but so she can't move around too much. Call her a very short distance to the fist but don't make the angle of flight too steep or the inexperienced bird will not come. A low branch and a low angle of flight. Try this several times, increasing the distance so that the bird is confident in the tree. Perhaps try another tree – the whole thing could get very exciting! As with all birds, call into the wind.

Dummy Rabbit

The next thing to do, if you want to, is to introduce the owl to the dummy rabbit. Put the owl on her normal flying post and place the dummy rabbit about 10ft (3m) away on the grass. Put a small piece of meat on the dummy as an instant reward, and now pull it very slowly past the owl. If the bird flies down and lands next to it, then stop and see if she will step onto the rabbit, or even grab it, you might have to give it a tiny pull to encourage the bird. We also have a rather nice dummy rat which we use for the smaller owls. If it doesn't work don't worry, you can try putting the owl on the floor next to it and see if you get a reaction. What we often do is teach the owl to fly down to small pieces of meat thrown on the

ground, as well as working to the fist and to pieces on the flying post. This will attract the bird to other areas, as well as the fist, and will make introducing the dummy bunny or rat all the easier. As a last resort give the dummy to the bird, showing her where the meat is and letting her take the meat off as a reward, thus giving the bird the idea the dummy is edible.

The rabbit may take several days to achieve, but if you persevere it will work, I promise! Once the bird is walking after the dummy it is only a matter of time and patience before she will take it in fast flight. I often continue with training with the dummy work once I have the bird loose, after making sure that the bird is not frightened by the dummy.

When the owl is coming well to the fist or to a piece of meat on the perch, coming out of a low branch of a tree and appears to be obedient at 50yd (45m), fly her free. You have no idea how many people come to us at the Centre and say that they are not sure when to fly their bird free: she has been coming well on a creance for two months or even more and they still have not let her free. I normally expect to get any bird, with the exception of the true hawks and the eagles, loose in two weeks. There is no point in keeping them on a line once they are coming the full length on the creance straightaway to the whistle. Get the bird loose and have some fun!

It is up to you whether or not you use a bell. We don't as we need to show silent flight at the Centre, and the bell spoils that. However, a lightweight Indian leg bell is fine, but should be put on in the early days of training, long before the owl goes loose.

Flying Loose

Rule number one, choose good weather: no wind; no rain; no fog. Rule two, have someone with you the first couple of times. Rule three, fly the bird loose at least two hours before dark so you have time to retrieve her. Rule four, don't panic! Get ready in the normal way: meat ready in your bag; flying perch in the car if you need one. Into the pen, owl to the fist for a tiny piece of meat, take hold of the hunting straps. We do not bother with putting on the mews jesses and leash and swivel as we are flying our birds on our own premises, but we do if we are going away anywhere. If you have to travel to your flying ground, jess up, etc. Take the bird into your weighing room and check she is the right weight. Either walk to your flying area or put the bird in the travelling box and drive.

Behave in all ways just the same as you have done on every other day. Pop the bird on the post or perch with the creance on and ask for a short jump to the fist. If all goes well, take off the creance, the swivel, the mews jesses and leave only the hunting straps. Put the bird back on the perch and fly her loose. Don't overdo it on the first day. I would probably not use the dummy rabbit or rat today unless the owl really likes to catch it. Once you have finished after all has gone well – which it should do – put the bird back into the pen and go and congratulate yourself *after* you have put away your bag, glove etc and checked that your bird is OK. The welfare of the bird always comes before your own.

It is very rare for things to go wrong on the first day loose. It tends to be later when you are starting to get careless and try flying the bird on a day when the weather is too windy or wet, or you get the weight of the bird wrong, or you are not concentrating enough. So beware of this and watch what you are doing at all times. Try to fly your bird on a daily basis, although you should avoid windy days until the bird is really secure in her training and you feel confident.

For those of you who are just going to fly your owl for fun, you are now in possession of a trained owl. You can continue to fly her in the same way, see if you can take her for walks with you by getting her to follow from tree to tree or along fence lines, but be careful and keep an eye on the bird at all times and also on whatever else you might meet on your walk. If you see a large group of people coming, or horse riders, or dogs that you do not know are safe with your bird, call her to the fist and move out of the way. In fact, control your bird in much the same way you would control your dog (or at least I hope you would) when out for a walk. Be very careful to avoid going near roads, owls are very prone to being hit by cars and a trained owl flying across a road is very vulnerable. If you are going to fly your owl in several different places, or train her to follow on, then it *is* probably a good idea to put a bell on her. We don't bother here at The National Birds of Prey Centre because on the few times the owls have gone out of the field all we have to do is watch to see where all the local Crows, Rooks,

Magpies and Jays are going nuts, usually at one tree. If we then get over to that tree, there will be a very upset owl, usually only too pleased to see you and have the corvids chased away.

Hunting

If you are going to hunt with your bird, I would use telemetry rather than a bell. This would allow the owl to use her natural talent of silent flight to the best advantage in the hunting field.

Your hunting bird will be trained in exactly the same way as any other owl, you will just carry the training on a little farther. You should do a little more work with the dummy bunny. Put the bird in a tree, having set the bunny in place first in some cover, then sit for a while before moving the dummy. Try twitching the rabbit to see if a tiny movement can get the owl's attention and once she is concentrating then run with the rabbit and keep making it more difficult for the owl to catch as she gets more confident. But teach the bird that you expect her to sit for a while before the rabbit will move. You should be feeding your hunting owl on rabbit by now so that she knows what one looks, tastes and feels like.

Next use a real, dead rabbit as the lure instead of the dummy rabbit. You should let the owl have a feed on the dead rabbit to encourage her. Take the owl to different places to fly so that she is used to different surroundings, use the dummy or the dead (fresh) rabbit in different situations so that the bird starts to look for it. Without doubt the owl is going to be much happier hunting at a more natural time of day, so early dawn and dusk would be the most appropriate times, particularly in the early stages when you are trying to catch something for the first time.

Owls need time so take your now trained and very obedient bird to a good site where you know if you sit quietly, rabbits will come out. Put the owl in a tree with a good vantage point, and just sit and wait. This is where your sitting and waiting before pulling the bunny will help. This is also where your fieldcraft comes into play. Remember, if you don't know where the quarry is or when it will be about you will not make a good hunter. Now is when you need to know good places to go.

Early summer is the best time as there are young rabbits about. You will just have to experiment here and see if you can get your owl to wait long enough for the rabbits to come out. If you have done enough work with the dummy and dead rabbits then eventually you will be rewarded, but don't be disappointed if it doesn't work the first time. Come to that, don't be disappointed if you don't catch anything for a month, keep trying and eventually you will succeed. If you are finding that the owl will not go after a rabbit from a tree, try her from your fist, or even from the ground if the view is good enough, for example, on a rise in the ground or on top of a hill. Make sure the weather is good and still on the days that you try. If you are not getting any interest from the bird then try bringing her weight down a little lower than you normally would fly her, but remember to put it back up as soon as you have succeeded. You may find that you have to fly pretty close to dark before the owl will start to chase things but once she gets the idea you should be able to try in daylight.

The first time you catch a rabbit go in fairly quickly, without upsetting the bird, and if the quarry is not dead, dispatch it quickly and cleanly while it is still in the owl's feet. You should not take the quarry away from the bird on her first kill. Without fail you should let the bird feed on it, until she is full. This could take quite a long time so don't be impatient. If you remove the first few kills you will find that the bird becomes less interested in hunting. Once you have caught, say, ten rabbits you can start taking them away. If you have fed your bird up on her kill you must now take her home and you will probably find that she is overweight for the next day or two. You will not be able to fly her again straightaway, let her come back down to weight and then try hunting again. Only by persevering will you succeed in hunting with an owl.

Breeding

This is not meant to be a book on captive breeding of owls. Most of what I wrote on captive breeding in *Falconry* is relevant to breeding any species of birds of prey including the owls. However, I will cover a little on keeping owls for breeding and I would suggest you get the other book as well which will tell you all about artificial incubation and rearing. The techniques I use are the same for the owls as for every other species: same incubators, same temperature; same brooders; same feeding regime; same everything.

Firstly, remember that if you are going to breed with owls you can't go into the pens with them and play around, you can't fly them, they are just for breeding and to be left alone to get on with it.

Secondly, it is a waste of your time and money, and also morally wrong, to breed birds for which there is no *suitable* market. You could breed lots of Barn Owls or eagle owls, sell them to pet shops and garden centres to be sold on again to anyone who wants a bird regardless of their experience or suitability. If you want to do that then I'd advise you to keep well away from me, I consider that sort of behaviour to be despicable. So if you want to breed owls, choose those that are either useful, rare or suitably needed in some way. I can't give you a species list as it will change as more birds are bred successfully. Again, the answer to that is research. Find out what the market needs. Have a look in *Cage and Aviary Birds*, the weekly magazine that advertises birds of prey and owls for sale. You will then see what is for sale in large numbers and thus there is a glut on the market. Looking at the Zoos' Surplus Lists is quite useful as well.

Once you have decided what you want, you have to build a suitable breeding aviary for your birds. Go back to Chapter 2 and see what type of aviary was recommended. A decent-sized pen with a service passage at back or side (service passage to have concrete floor and a decent sized door to push wheelbarrows through); three sides solid, one open with weldmesh of some sort; completely covered roof in either Onduline or fibre/concrete with plenty of roof lights (owls need light as much as any other species); a large nest ledge or nest box depending on the species (if you are trying to breed from the larger species it is probably better to give them a large open-topped box on the ground, or at least not high off the ground). The young of these large species often hurt themselves falling out of higher nest ledges when they are starting to get adventurous. Many of the large species often nest on the ground in the wild. I suggest an open-topped box as you can then see what is happening from a spy-hole in the service passage wall. Locate a built-in bath on the front low wall with an access door for cleaning. Place a nice deep fine gravel floor on top of hardcore. Tree-like perches of a large enough diameter for the birds to perch comfortably should be dug into the floor of the aviary. We also try to put in a couple of large rocks for the bigger owls as they seem to like using them. A removable feeding drawer for keeping food off the floor will make cleaning easy.

The nest box, or ledge, should have at least 4in (10cm) of mixed peat (Irish moss peat) and pea gravel on the floor (6in (15cm) or more for the medium and large species). Sand is also very good. Owls don't build nests, they dig a scrape in the ground and so you need a surface they can do this in happily, but deep enough that they won't get through to the hardcore below.

Recommended *minimum* sizes for breeding owl pens:

- Large Owls, eg Great Horned Owls, McKinders Eagle Owls etc 10x16x8ft (3x4.8x2.4m)
- Medium Owls, eg Bengal Eagle Owls, African Spotted Eagle Owls 10x10x8ft (3x3x2.4m)
  Small Owls, eg Little Owls, Scops Owls 6x10x6ft (1.8x3x1.8m)

Once you have the aviary prepared, the nest box/ledge in place, your food supply and vet organised, your equipment – the net and glove – ready, now you can get your owls. You will either get them from a private breeder or a collection. I would strongly advise against a dealer or a pet shop as you must have realised by now. Make sure that you have a pair. The size difference between the males and females can be quite obvious with the larger owls but much less so with the smaller ones. If you are worried either get the owner to guarantee what sex they are, or you can have them surgically sexed by a good vet. You should also try, wherever possible, to get a pair that are unrelated. With some species this is really difficult but breeding from related birds should be avoided as it will lead to problems in the long run. You will have to be just as careful buying a pair of owls for breeding as for any other requirement but you don't need hand-reared birds, in fact it is better to have them parent-reared if you can.

Unless you are going to go into breeding birds of prey and/or owls in numbers I would suggest that you do not go in for incubators, brooders and all the rest of the expensive equipment that you need if you are going to double clutch. All this is very time-consuming and really not worth it in the long run. It's much nicer to have a pair of birds and watch them go through all the pre-nuptial agreements: food passing; hooting at one another; digging a nest scrape; frightening you to death because they might go off their food during laying! Most birds can manage to hatch and rear their own young as long as you have got the aviary and nest site right, good food and enough of it during the breeding season and, most importantly, you must *leave the birds alone*. Don't keep going into the pen and disturbing them.

Once the birds have young you must increase the amount of food slowly at first, because tiny young do not consume a great deal but once they start to really grow after about a week to ten days you will be amazed at how much food they will eat, especially the larger species. Try to feed twice a day, morning and evening, so that there is fresh food for the young most of the time and feed a varied diet at all times. The only way to know if you are giving enough is to feed too much, ie have a little left over. This is where your feed drawer will come in really handy as the food should be left on there and you can remove it and clean it regularly.

If you want to go into double clutching, incubating with artificial incubators, hand-rearing and all the rest of the more intensive breeding methods, buy *Falconry* and follow the instructions in there. But unless you have a rare, and much wanted, species just let the owls get on with it and have the pleasure of watching the young grow up, play in the aviary and generally have a good time. You can leave the young with the parents until about September/October time but, if possible, remove them by then, giving the parent birds time to have a break before starting the cycle again.

As a breeder the onus is now on you to make sure that any young you produce and either sell, exchange or give away, go to good, knowledgeable homes with decent aviaries and food supplies.

CHAPTER SEVEN
FALCONS

There is not really anything difficult in training falcons, in fact, the larger ones often train a lot easier than other family groups. One of the most difficult things to learn to do well is swing a lure and this doesn't really matter as long as you make sure you don't damage a bird. For a hunting falcon you are only going to use the lure to call her in after a missed kill. A demonstration falcon requires much more thought and skill which is why there are a lot of rather poor demonstration falcons about!

What Sort of Falcon?

As a beginner, you must avoid any of the small falcons such as Kestrels. Merlins, Hobbies and others that might become available later like Red-headed Merlins, Aplomado Falcons and so on. Some of these make excellent lure birds, some good hunting birds, but *all* make dreadful beginner's birds because of their size and weight, too easy to kill.

Kestrels don't make good hunting birds or good lure birds, they make quite fun birds to take for a walk or to have as a pet and, with a lot of hard work, you can get them to hover. Generally they are first class at coming to the fist and sitting in trees and not a lot else!

So for a beginner wanting a falcon what else is there? Well in the UK at the moment you have available Peregrines; Lanners; Sakers; Luggers; Prairies; New Zealand Falcons (occasionally) and Gyrs. And then there are hybrids.

Gyr Falcon
Forget about Gyrs as a beginner, as I very much doubt if you will want to spend that much on a bird that you are fairly likely to lose. They can be *very* temperamental and throw pretty good tantrums.

A juvenile male Lanner, known as a Lanneret – Hector, aged 1

Peregrine Falcon
I would not waste time with a Peregrine either. These days they are very easy to get, many people are breeding them but they are wasted unless you either fly them at grouse on a decent moor or at partridges on large open stubble, in which case you will need a very good pointing dog too. You can fly the females or large males at Rooks although I much prefer to kill Crows, but then I don't like Crows (or Magpies). By all means get a Peregrine if you have to, but they are very easy to lose as they will go a long way after quarry and they are not really a beginner's bird.

Saker
Sakers are interesting birds and they are pretty easy to train. I have not had one that I would call temperamental but none of them liked travelling in the boxes very much, particularly prior to being flown. They were not so bad travelling home once fed. Some people say they are liable to 'straight-line it' occasionally, ie disappear in a straight line refusing to turn when called in to the lure. The Saker is a very greedy bird and her weight easily creeps up daily, with the bird behaving herself beautifully until one day she is well overweight and something upsets her or the weather conditions are wrong then off she goes. I have flown a number of Sakers and apart from the fact that they all tend to sit down after a while, probably because we have so many trees around, I like them a lot. They are strong fliers, very willing, some will get up height straightaway although the hovering is a bit of a drag. A male Saker might make a beginner's bird if you can't get a Lanner but don't go for a female as they go further and are a little more scary. I would also consider flying the Saker at ground game such as small rabbits or pheasants as they prefer ground game to aerial game.

Prairie Falcon
Prairies, well just how much patience have you really got because, boy, you will need it for one of

these! Because of their, let's say 'a touch difficult' temperament, they do not make a good beginner's bird. They are, however, much underrated falcons. They have a braveness and tenacity that you are unlikely to find in many birds. The size difference between the males and females is great – the males are almost half the size of the females. Prairies will take a large variety of game from small birds, such as starlings (this is usually the males), through to pheasants and even rabbits and once you know what you are doing and have plenty of time and even more patience I would suggest you try one. But as a bird for someone starting up, don't do it, she/he will just depress you!

Lugger

Luggers, like the Prairie, are temperamental, but I have had some very good fliers and I have also caught stuff with them by accident. The ironic thing is that, with the new DNA testing to ascertain the taxonomy (who is related to who) of falcons, the Lugger is closely related to the Gyr Falcon which I find very amusing as so many people are so rude about the species. They make a reasonably good beginner's bird as long as you give them plenty of manning. They will fly well to the lure and can be entered on Moorhens if you can flush them (get a decent dog – a Labrador!), Magpies if you enter them early on young ones, or Starlings for the males.

Lanner

Lanners are, without doubt, the large falcon with the nicest temperament that I know of and this alone makes them a good beginner's bird. They will hunt if you persevere and don't make the mistake of trying to compare them with other species of falcons. They make excellent lure birds and will teach you a great deal. Either sex can be trained but much more care will be needed with the weight of the male as they can be very small. Just to give you an idea of the variation: I have had male Lanners that have flown at $13\frac{1}{2}$oz (380g) and ones at 1lb 5oz (595g), a difference of 8oz (215g). I have had females that have flown at 1lb 3oz (540g) and ones at 1lb 9oz (708g). So as you can see, you have to be very careful. A 13oz (370g) Lanner is very small and can go underweight and get ill or even die on you very easily. That is why I would suggest that an inexperienced person tries a female.

New Zealand Falcon

They are few and far between and not really suitable for a beginner. I know of several very experienced falconers who have been driven to distraction by them, however, the New Zealand Falcon is a very versatile and interesting bird. They all originate from Dr Nick Fox's breeding project and for any really good information on them you should contact him. I have only flown one for demonstration here.

Hybrids

Hybrids are birds that are half one species and half another. I have to admit that I still have mixed feelings about cross-breeding. Having said that, I have flown five Peregrine/Saker hybrids and they are all absolutely brilliant and I love them all. I am still flying two and will be disappointed if Martin Jones and I don't breed any between us this year. However, I am not in favour of silly crosses like Merlin/Kestrel or American Kestrel/Gyr. Also I can not see the point of such crosses as Lanner/Lugger.

Some people are adamantly against cross-breeding but I look at the breeding mankind has done over thousands of years which really has done very little harm, certainly to wild populations. I think that if certain rules are followed then hybrids are acceptable. If these rules are thrown aside and people start to behave as some dog and cat breeders do then that would be a great shame in the true sense of the word. If only Labrador people had said: 'We will not breed with any dog that has hip problems', for example, then I would not have Salix, the most beautiful Labrador dog in the world whose hips are not good and may get a great deal worse as he gets older. But now it is too late as the problem is probably latent in the breed and can come out in any generation. If that happened in birds that would be wrong, so we have to be very careful. The rules should be these:
- The hybrids should not affect the wild population.
- The hybrids should be of good healthy genetic stock.

Having said all that, hybrids are probably not the birds for beginners. They can be very exciting birds, a little too exciting for beginners, so save one of these for a second falcon when you have a little more experience. Go for a female Lanner as first choice or male as second, or a female Lugger then a male and finally, if you choose none of the others, a male Saker.

Housing

The same type of housing described in Chapter 2 is suitable for falcons. Because of the different type of perch used a tethered falcon does not need as much room as a similarly sized hawk. A bow perch allows the leash, and therefore the bird, to move 4ft (1.2m) further than the block would allow the falcon to do. However, as you are going to aim to have your bird living free in the pen once she is trained and really tame, you will find that falcons need as much space as the hawks because of their long, pointed primaries. They are also not as agile in a pen as the hawks are so they always need more space.

Follow the instructions in Chapter 2, build well, build attractively, build to last and there you have it. All the falcons, particularly Gyrs and Peregrines, are susceptible to bumblefoot so it is advisable to cover all perches with Astroturf.

Food

Many falcons do not like rats or mice. We use day-old chicks, grown-on chicks to five weeks, quail and beef for our falcons and they seem to do and look very well on that diet. For feeding on the fist we use beef, but under no circumstances is that the only food type that the birds get. We use it because it is nice and tough and is acceptable to our visitors; half a quail will do, as will a rabbit leg. We almost never feed chick on the fist, preferring to give it to the birds at the end of the day when they can feed peacefully in the early evening. We usually put the vitamin supplement on the beef as we find that we can see the birds are eating it all.

Some people say that you should only feed your bird on the fist, well that is pretty out of date. Once your falcon is trained and tame and able to go loose in your pen, it is perfectly acceptable to put food in for her.

Finding Your Falcon

The same rules apply for getting any bird. Without any shadow of doubt, unless you want a semen-doning male falcon, or an egg-laying

A Hybrid Peregrine/Saker, Kilbreck, aged 3½ years. This is one of my favourite birds: they are marvellous fliers

female who will accept AI, you do not want an imprint falcon. Don't let anyone persuade you otherwise or you will regret it. Even the best imprinted bird can be noisy, aggressive with food and often will only catch one prey item per day as you cannot afford to upset them. I wouldn't have an imprinted bird for flying even if you paid me a considerable sum of money.

Badly imprinted falcons are even worse as they will scream all day (the noise of a falcon screaming constantly has to be heard to believed). They will mantle badly on the lure or on quarry, they can be extremely aggressive with their handler and are generally horrid. Sadly they are often advertised at a cheap price and even then I would strongly advise against one. Look for a nice

LEFT

Saker (a juvenile, bred at the Centre). I have always liked Sakers, and they are nice birds to handle. But they are very greedy and tend to lie about how starving they are, and so it is very easy to push their weight up too high too quickly. When this happens they will suddenly disappear on you, covering a lot of miles in a short space of time. It can take a while to retrieve them as their weight has to drop before they will respond and come back

RIGHT

Prarie Falcons like this 'just bathed' young male are very temperamental and not for the inexperienced. They are very inclined to throw tantrums and be totally unreasonable about life in general, but if you have the patience and experience to train one, they are excellent hunting birds. The females are considerably larger than the males

BELOW

This is Dogger, my juvenile male Lugger Falcon. He has come close to getting strangled on many an occasion! Like the Prairie the Lugger is prone to be temperamental, but is less use as a hunting bird. Having had three first-class Luggers in the past, I keep hoping to train one as good, but unfortunately none of those I have bred have turned out to be brilliant

parent-reared, well-adjusted bird and you will have years of pleasure, find a bad one and I guarantee that you will not want to keep her for long and in the end you would probably pay someone to take her away.

If you know a good breeder who has a good reputation, then order a bird from him or her. You may well find that you need to join a waiting list very early on to be assured of a bird. And on that subject, please remember that things don't always go to plan with breeding and very often a breeder will not be as successful as he or she hopes. Very soon I am going to charge £10 extra per phone call to those people who call unnecessarily, throughout the breeding season, wanting to know what is happening! As a breeder of birds of prey I do my best to produce birds for all those who order them but occasionally things go wrong. For example, this year one of my normally very good breeding pairs of Harrises decided to lay each egg from a 14ft swinging perch and the eggs just don't seem to have got the idea yet! Result, only one baby instead of the normal five or six, and six broken eggs. That's the way it goes occasionally.

Most falcons should be ready to train in about August and so that is when you should plan to get your bird.

Collecting Your New Falcon

Have your nice collecting box carefully carpeted. Don't put a towel on the floor of the box as this does not give a stable surface and will probably be rolled up in a ball in one corner of the box by the time you get home. Falcons are very good at giving themselves self-inflicted wounds to their feet. Remember that falcons probably have more bumblefoot than any other family of birds of prey. Always make sure that they are not in a position to puncture their own feet.

When you collect your falcon, having made sure that the breeder is expecting you, have your jesses etc with you if you are able to jess the bird up straightaway. The first thing we do here at the Centre, when we catch up falcons, is to take the tips off their talons with a pair of electrical wire cutters, usually while the bird is still in the net as this holds the talons away from the feet. Only the tips need be cut and they will soon sharpen up again. It just stops them puncturing themselves during the initial travelling and training period. If

the breeder does not do this, do it yourself when you remove the bird from the box on your return home. When the breeder has collected the bird for you, check her over physically paying particular attention to the feet. When you are happy either jess and then box the bird or just box her if the breeder has not got the time to assist you. Under no circumstances should any bird be wearing a leash while in a box. It takes very little for the leash to get tangled around the bird and injure or even kill her.

Settling In

On arriving home, having taken care travelling so that the bird does not overheat in the box, take your bird out in a safe room that is dimly lit. If there are windows make sure they are closed with the curtains drawn. Have someone there to help you jess and bell the bird. As stated before, I like to put the tail bell on at this stage as the bird is going to be stressed anyway, so you might as well get everything done at one time.

Make sure that you have everything ready before getting the bird out of the box. If you intend hooding your falcon, you must have the hood available from the first day that you start training. Slide the door up enough to see where the bird is and then, with your gloved hand, try to catch hold of both legs. You can put in both hands and try to get them around the bird's body and legs but this is more difficult if you are not experienced. Once you have both legs, and try to do this as quickly as possible, open the door the whole way or get your assistant to do it for you and bring the bird out quickly, holding her towards the middle of the room where her wings cannot touch anything. Then either you or your helper can take the bird's wings, fold them as they should be, then wrap the falcon gently in a tea towel, leaving the feet and tail free. Jess with Aylmeri of False Aylmeri, put on the swivel, turn the falcon so that you or your assistant can get to the tail and put on the tail bell (see Chapter 4). Then put the leash on and the hood and let the bird go onto the fist. Now weigh the bird; chart down the weight because you will need to remember it as you are not going to touch the bird for about five to seven days.

Take the bird to your smart pen, which is squeaky clean with sand on the floor, where a block awaits your bird. Tie the leash to the block

with the falconer's knot. Gently persuade the hooded falcon to step back onto the block by lifting her tail over the back of the block and pressing the legs against the block with your fist held low. When the bird is on the block, take off your glove and put it in your pocket, undo the hood braces with both bare hands and gently remove it, while stepping back slow and low. Leave the bird alone until the next day. Alternatively you can put the bird out on a quiet grass lawn for the first few hours while she fights the jesses, but you must be around to keep an eye on her and there must be no children, cats, dogs or the like around for those first few hours while the bird sorts herself out. Under no circumstances should a bird be left on the lawn after about 6pm in the summer, and earlier in winter, as you risk foxes coming in and killing her. After that time the bird should be tethered in her pen safe from all dangers.

Keep an eye on the new arrival from the front of the pen, through the wire, but don't disturb her other than going in once a day to throw in some food, making sure it lands within reach. The bird will probably not feed for a couple of days but make sure that you are giving her food that she has been used to having. It is a good idea to check with the breeder as to what food he or she uses. On about day three your new falcon should

PUTTING A HOODED BIRD ON THE PERCH

1 *When putting a hooded bird on a perch, lift the tail and drop it gently over the back of the perch*

2 *Press the back of the legs gently against the perch and the bird will step back*

be sitting well on the block, getting back on when she bates off and feeding from the food that you are throwing in. After five to seven days the bird should have settled well, be fairly used to her new surroundings and be ready to start training.

Handling

On the day you decide to start handling your bird don't throw her any food. You may be asking yourself why you should leave the bird for several days before starting training. The answer is stress. Your new falcon will have been caught up out of what she considered to be her home, removed from parents or siblings, man-handled, boxed, travelled, taken out, jessed, tethered, put in a new home and so on. Add trying to tame and train onto all this and it is just much kinder to let the bird settle to all the new traumas in her life before starting training. It will also make the training much quicker.

Before you try picking up your bird put on your falconry bag and have a nice piece of meat, or half quail or rabbit leg, well slashed, ready in one of the pockets. Weigh the food first so you know how much you gave the bird and what that amount of that type of food does to the bird's weight. The first day you pick up your bird she will not be pleased to see you so go in quickly, run your bare hand up the leash and, holding the jesses with your gloved hand, lift the bird off the ground to the fullest length of the leash. Put the jesses into safety position, undo the leash and stand up quickly, moving to the middle of the pen so that the wings won't hit anything. During this time the falcon will be hanging upside-down. Put the jesses in the correct position down the centre of your hand, pull the leash through so that half of it is through the swivel, then wind the halved leash around your little finger, tightly, and then around the next finger, loosely, making sure all the ends meet. Then close your hand into a fist and keep it that way. All this should be done as quickly as possible so that if the falcon is bating

PICKING UP A HOODED FALCON

1 Lifting a hooded bird off the block

2 As you lift the glove, the bird will step up

RIGHT & INSET
Blewitt, who sadly died last year at the age of 17, was probably one of the best-known Lanners in the UK. His high stoops (see inset) at the Game Fair for 12 years were legendary. Lanners are the best falcons for beginners; their uncomplicated nature, steady temperament and versatility make them very pleasant to work with. If flown in the right terrain and at the right quarry they will make hunting birds. Various friends of mine in Zimbabwe catch numerous Francolin, which are similar to our Partridge. They are, however, less easy to enter because they are very bright birds and will not chase if they don't think they can kill easily

and moving about, the leash does not get tangled around the wings. Once you have the jesses and leash secure, lift the falcon up onto the fist. I suggest that you do this from behind the falcon, not putting your hand onto her breast as falcons bite and bite hard. Pick her up by lifting from just above the tail and you should not get bitten.

Once the bird is sitting up you should hood her. The first time you hood a falcon it is pretty easy (unless you are dealing with a Prairie Falcon)! As the bird does not know what is happening you can slip the hood on over the head before she realises what is going on. I like to slip the hood over the bird's head in a rolling motion

HOODING

1 Slip the hood gently but swiftly over the head – but don't rush

5 Leave for a second or two. It is vital to have a falcon that will sit still with the braces undone

2 & 3 Use a rolling motion, following the shape of the falcon's head

6 Use one hand and your teeth to open or close the hood

4 Tap the hood into place with your fingers

7 Don't hang about here: whether you're putting on the hood or taking it off, do up or undo the braces quickly. Never remove the hood straightaway: leave it on for a count of 20

OPPOSITE
A hooded Lanner falcon: Hogger, aged 3½

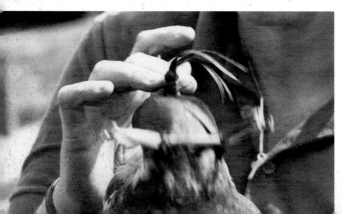

following the shape of the head, then I tap it gently into place with one finger and do up the braces with one hand and my teeth. Hooding is not easy. I can't make it any easier by describing it, that can and will only come as you practise. The important things to remember are that the hood should fit well and should not be overused. I know there are still people who put a hood on their new falcon when they first get her and don't take it off again for several days except for trying to feed the bird. This is an awful thing to do and gains nothing in the training of a bird. Some people even try to feed a new bird through the hood: this is a bloody silly thing to do as you will then have a falcon who is always tearing at the glove while hooded in case there is food she can't see. The hood should only be used for short periods early on and I strongly disapprove of leaving a bird hooded for hours at any stage of her life. Hoods can be very useful but they can also be misused and have killed birds. However, having said that, the hood must be used from the *first* day of training. If you leave it for three of four days before introducing the hood you will find that the bird starts to get used to you and will be concentrating on the hood and will learn to avoid it. Start on the first day and you will be fine.

Once you have hooded your bird after the first pick up, take her out of the aviary, and go and weigh her in your weighing room – don't forget to lock the door. Chart down the weight. Go outside to a nice comfy seat in the garden, sit down, put the meat on the glove, holding it between your thumb and fingers, and undo the braces of the hood but *don't remove it straightaway*. Leave it on for a couple of minutes. If you take the hood off straightaway you will eventually have a bird that pulls back every time you touch the hood which is a real drag, so always wait a few seconds before taking the hood off after you have 'struck the braces'.

You will need to encourage your bird to feed by touching the meat, touching her feet and generally showing her where the meat is. We usually find that our falcons will feed on the fist the first day we start handling, they also learn to get back onto the fist after bating on that first day. This is because the birds have been tethered for a week, or sometimes more, because they have learned to accept the jesses, have got used to seeing us around and generally are much more settled than when they first were removed from the aviary.

The stress is far less and the training should go along very easily.

Once the bird has eaten as much as she likes, try gently stroking her breast with the hood. Then put the hood on, leave it for a couple of seconds and take it off again. Do this several times, occasionally do up the braces, then undo them but leave the hood in place. By the time you have done this for five minutes, the bird should be getting more used to the idea. If you do this at every training session for the next ten days, you will have a bird that is good to hood. Now and again you should leave the hood on for five minutes so that the bird gets used to longer periods. Man the bird, that is sit with it unhooded on your fist after it has eaten for about an hour, and then hood her up again and put her back on her perch in the aviary. Unhood her gently, moving away slow and low. You always want to end a training session on a good note.

Jumping to the Fist

If the bird has not eaten do not feed her and then the next day do the same thing all over again. Pick up, weigh, feed, man, hood practice, put back down. Once the bird has fed on the fist for two or three days you should try to get her to jump to the fist.

It is better to do this on a still day and try to use a post rather than a bar for the bird to sit on. On a bar they will often run up and down rather than jump, on a post they can't do this. If there is a breeze, always work the bird into the wind. Pick the bird up in the normal way, never forgetting safety position with the jesses, before getting them and the leash and swivel into the correct position. Weigh her. By this time you will not need to slash the meat as the bird will be pulling well for herself, in fact you could do with a fairly tough piece of meat so that she does not get too much to eat while the training session is going on. Pull the leash through until the button is against the swivel, tie the other end to your glove so that the bird cannot get loose should she bate away from you while on the post. Place the unhooded bird onto the post, get your piece of meat out, put it into your gloved hand and hold your hand slightly higher than the post and just out of reach of the falcon. You will probably find that the bird will try to lean forwards and grab the food – let her do it the first time as this encourages them.

The next time she must jump. She is far less likely to do this if you are holding your hand too low. Birds always prefer to jump to a higher point than a lower one. Hold your fist at right-angles to your body so that the bird is seeing space on the other side of the fist (rather than your chest). Try this for about five minutes, if she does not show any signs of wanting to jump by then, leave it. Pick the bird up off the post, with the meat, but then remove the food and don't feed her, just man and hood practice and return to the block. By this time you can be walking around with the bird on the fist, unhooded. Walk slowly and gently and persevere until the bird stops bating at all and sundry – then you are beginning to get somewhere!

If the bird jumps, swiftly put her back on the post after a couple of mouthfuls and try again a little further away. You are aiming at three to four jumps in this session, ending up with a full leash length. When taking meat away from any bird, wait until she has taken a pull and is swallowing that and then quickly and firmly, but not roughly or violently, pull the meat through the bottom of your hand and put it straightaway into your bag. Don't wave it about, get it out of sight as soon as possible. Put the bird back on the perch gently each time. You may find that the bird is a little sticky-footed but if you are patient she will learn to relax her grip. If, on the other hand, you are too fast and rough, you will teach the bird to be sticky-footed for the rest of her life. Patience is the key word.

Man, hood and be with the bird for at least an hour per day and preferably more. You can also start taking her into the house in the evenings but make sure you sit in a quiet part of the room and put newspaper on the floor below where you and the bird are sitting!

Continue doing this until the bird jumps well to the fist the full leash length, I usually do it for two days. Then move on to the next stage. By this time, now the bird is jumping to the fist, you can start to make your approach to your bird to pick her up from the perch in the aviary very much more slow and careful. You want to get to the stage where the bird is not bating away from you but, instead, is beginning to look forward to your arrival. So next time you want to pick the bird up prior to training her, give yourself about half an hour extra and go in really slow and low waving the pick-up piece to attract the falcon's attention.

End up by kneeling down by the block and see if you can get the bird to jump to the fist. If she has bated away from you, sit back on your heels, away from the block and see if the bird will fly back onto her perch, if not, entice her with a small piece of meat, put on the block, where it can be seen. Give the bird time, and sit quietly, eventually she will go back onto the block and now that you are already in position, you will find that she will be much more likely to jump to the fist. If she does, let her sit for a couple of seconds and then remove the meat and put it back on the block – try this several times. Then, returning the bird to the block, and at this stage you will not have untied her, get up slowly and walk away. Then return waving the meat and the bird should allow you to approach more easily this time. Go through this process several times and by the end of it you should find that the falcon will be more settled at your approach. Do this each day from now on so that eventually you can approach the bird without meat; remember, though, this takes several weeks to achieve. The training of a bird of prey, particularly a falcon, is very quick, the taming takes much longer and is usually achieved after the bird is training and flying free.

You may find that after spending this much time getting the bird to come to you off the block, that she will have eaten too much to be keen for a training session. If this is so, then just take her out, walk her around and man her for a couple of hours as this will not be time wasted.

Further Training

The next step is to take your falcon to the area where you intend flying her free on a regular basis. You will need an open area with as few trees as possible. You should also avoid, like the plague, any areas with telegraph poles within about 1/2 mile (1km). A telegraph pole is absolutely ideal for teaching a young falcon to sit down and, once you have managed to do that, you will find that the bird will enjoy sitting down for the rest of her flying life! If we have a bird that sits down here, on a regular basis, she leaves my employ as I am not interested in falcons that sit down. The occasional slip-up is just about acceptable but only three or four times a year and even then there has to be a good reason. If you train your bird in a good area and you never work her too hard in the early stages, then she should never learn to sit down. If she does, then nine times out of ten it will be your own fault. Our training field is not free of trees by any means but the flying area is fairly clear. You should not fly near pylons either as they can, and have, killed birds of prey.

For the first days of training you will need your flying area to have pretty short grass. If it is not your own land, ask the owner very nicely (be extra nice and give him or her a bottle of whiskey or whatever) if you can mow a 6ft (2m) wide and 100ft (30m) long strip for just ten days, ie about two mowings. You need this so that the creance does not get caught up in the grass or weeds. This can really upset a bird and so should be avoided. The area should be away from buildings, particularly those with large windows as falcons can easily fly into these, and away from a busy road so your young bird does not fly in front of an on-coming car. Not only will this probably write off your falcon but may even leave you liable for damages if a car hits the bird and then crashes. Come and have a look at our flying area at the Centre, it is far from ideal but we get some pretty good flying from the falcons.

You will need a good post, at the end of your training area, on which to place your falcon. Or you can make an A-frame perch which you can transport in the car and will make a good steady perch almost anywhere (see page 82).

Two or three days after your falcon has first jumped get your pick-up piece and your bag, your creance and a lure and you are ready for the next stage of the training. The lure we use is very simple and cannot hurt a falcon. I don't like the leather pads, or the solid bird-type lure, as some of my demonstration falcons hit the lure very hard and these can hurt a bird, so why take the risk? We use just a pair of wings usually from a magpie, partridge, moorhen or grouse. If you are intending to fly a certain quarry you can start the ball rolling by using a pair of wings from whatever it is you want to hunt. Of course, this is a little difficult of you want to fly a Saker at rabbits. I don't use pheasant, crow, duck or any of the larger wings because I swing a lure with a special style and I need short, rounded wings that will not catch the wind and 'helicopter' or spin round on the end of the swivel at the end of the lure line. We then put the wings back to back and tie them together with strong string, around the bones that hold the primaries, then, onto the knot of the string, we tie a tough piece of meat weighing about 2–3oz (60–90g). Run the long end of the string through the swivel on the end of the lure line and tie it to the short end of the string in a reef knot. This is our lure.

Go and pick up your falcon, gently, trying to get her to come to you from the block. Hood and weigh her then go to your training area. If you are very lucky this will be within walking distance of your home, remember, it is not good for the sport of falconry or the hobby of keeping birds of prey and owls to march through the middle of towns. We do not need to hide our heads in the sand or be ashamed of what we do, nevertheless, broad-casting where you train and fly a falcon to all and sundry could cause you endless problems. Keep a low profile when carrying birds around.

If it is raining or windy, don't do the following training session. During the entire period of the training of a bird, and particularly on the first few days flying free, avoid windy days as they are not good for young birds. If there is a slight breeze always call the bird into the wind. You should, therefore, check the direction of the prevailing winds before you mow your strip!

If you have to drive to your flying area you must now take great care. I would suggest that, at this stage, you do not use the box that you are going to build for travelling a trained diurnal bird of prey (which is different from the box you collected your bird in, see Chapter 3). Get someone else to have the hooded falcon on the fist or drive you to the flying area. In this way you or your helper can watch the bird to make sure she is not getting car sick and you don't have to try to get a semi-trained bird out of the travelling box. Start to use this box a little later on when the bird is tamer. You can always do some trial runs with the bird and the box in your weighing room. Place the bird into the box hooded and then unhood her. Give her a little titbit and then offer the glove with a pick-up piece and lift the bird out of the box. Always hold the bird slightly lower than the perch inside the box and this should stop the bird trying to bate towards the top of the door. If you practise this while the bird is still wearing her leash you will have control if the bird tries to fly out of the box but, as I have said before, never leave a leash on a boxed bird.

When you arrive at the flying ground, put up your A-frame perch while the bird is hooded on your fist and use the other arm for carrying the perch. You will find that eventually you get quite good at doing all sorts of things one-handed. If you have a post, ready and waiting, in the flying ground, so much the better. Unwind the leash from your fingers and put the swivel into safety position. While the leash is still on, tie on the creance with the normal falconer's knots. Then remove the leash. Fold it in half, twice, then loop it through itself around the strap of your bag. Walk, with the hooded falcon, about 20ft (6m) away from the post on the mown/short grass, throw the wound-up creance on the ground and then walk back to the post letting the creance unwind on the grass behind you. Unhood the falcon and put your hood in a safe pocket or on a hood block on your belt, not in the bag with your meat and lure. Put the falcon on the post or A-frame perch either by dropping your hand below the perch and encouraging the falcon to step onto the higher perch, or by gently lifting the tail over the back of the post and dropping the bird so that the legs are pressed against the post. She should step off backwards. Walk back to where the partly unwound creance lies, unwind a little more if you think you might need it, (in the same way you unwind the lure, ie from the centre of the stick rather than over one or other end) and put the remaining wound line, still on the stick, in your pocket. This will mean that whatever happens you will be in control of the line at all times. Call the bird to the fist over a short distance as you have been doing for the last couple of days but, remember, you are now in a different location so the bird might take a couple of minutes to settle down, or be very interested in looking at her new surroundings before concentrating on you and food. Once she has jumped a short distance, increase the distance to 5ft (1.5m) then to about 8ft (2.5m). If she does that readily then you are ready to try introducing the lure. Don't ask a young falcon to come to the fist any farther than 10ft (3m) as she will get up too much speed and find it difficult to stop.

Put the bird back on the post, and take the handle of your lure line out of the bag, leaving the meat end hidden in the bag. You should have made sure that, at all times, you put your pick-up piece in the opposite side of the bag to the lure. Undo the line by holding the handle with the line running between your second and third fingers and pulling the handle around with the line coming off from the middle. Don't pull the line over the end of the handle as this will twist the line before you even start. Once it is all undone, get a couple of large loops around the fingers of your gloved hand and close your hand into a fist, walk back from the falcon and pull the meat end out of the bag. This is when you find out if you left the pick-up piece in the wrong side! You will look very silly if the pick-up piece flies out of the bag and lands on the ground when you pull out your lure. This is particularly embarrassing once the bird is loose because she is just as likely to fly off, grab the pick-up and disappear into the blue leaving you feeling like a bit of a prat.

Swing the lure around a couple of times and drop it on the ground about 6ft (2m) in front of the falcon, *whistling as you do it*. Don't drop it too close or the angle of descent will be too great from the post/perch, and not too far away or the bird will not have the incentive or courage to come down.

It is a good idea to practise with your lure before trying this. Good lure swinging is an art and take years to get perfect. I can't describe how we do it on paper or even in photos. But as long as you can control the line, drop the lure within a foot of where you planned it to go and don't injure the bird, either by hitting it with the lure or by tearing it out of her feet if she catches you out, then don't worry. Practise using an old short sock, put a handful of sand or soil or gravel in the bottom and tie it to the swivel of your lure line. Position yourself where the bird can't see you and where you have space, and practise getting it out of the bag quickly, undoing and doing up the line quickly, swinging and dropping it in the required place. You will find that it is not as easy as it looks.

If the bird starts to bob her head and look interested, give the line a little twitch to move the lure, but it might take three or four minutes before the bird responds. You may find that swinging and dropping it again will stimulate the bird. If you have no reaction in five minutes, stop, then jump the bird a short distance to the fist but do not feed her. Hood her, take her home, man her, perhaps watch a film on the TV with her and then put her to bed back on her block in the pen.

If you do get a reaction don't be surprised if she lands next to the lure and walks in – this is perfectly normal for a young bird. Once she is on the lure, the next part of the training is *very* important, needs a great deal of patience and, if you screw up now, you will have a badly behaved falcon for the rest of her life. The pick-up, off the lure, is vital, the last thing you want is a bird that tries to carry either the lure or whatever she catches. So take your time and relax. You should be standing at the end of the lure line holding the stick. *Don't move* towards the bird at all until she takes the lure *in both feet* and starts *feeding*. When a bird takes the lure she usually has it in one foot. The other foot is then left free to push her off the ground in a take-off. Once she takes the lure, or the quarry, with both feet she has committed herself to feeding on the ground. Her stance will change and she will start to concentrate on the lure, now is the time to start 'making in' to give you a technical term. If the bird is not starting to eat, give the line a tiny pull until she starts to concentrate on the meat and not on either looking around or trying to fly. You should hold the line tight the whole time at this stage, it works quite well to put your foot on it as this keeps the line tight on the ground and makes it more difficult for the bird to take off with the lure.

At this stage the bird's natural instinct is cutting in, she knows that feeding in the open, on the ground, makes her vulnerable to other birds and animals stealing the food, or perhaps even trying to eat her. So all she wants to do is fly off with the food. You may find that this does not happen the first few times, but, instead, the bird starts to do it a little later in the training, but I don't think I have ever trained a falcon that did not try it eventually. You must nip this habit in the bud. Once the bird has started to feed, and hold the meat with both feet, slowly move around at the end of the line until you are looking at the falcon from the front. Every time she puts her head down to feed move forward a step. Those of you who are as old as I am will remember a game at school called grandmother's footsteps – this is the game you are playing now! For those of you who aren't old enough: ask a grandmother! When the bird looks up: freeze; if she looks like she might fly: freeze. When you get to within about 6ft (2m), kneel down slowly and, bending low so that you don't loom over the bird, gently offer the bird a tiny titbit of meat on your gloved hand. When she takes it, move your hand away again. Do this three times. By the time you do it for the fourth time the bird will be leaning towards you, so this time you have the full pick-up in your gloved hand. Place this directly on top of the lure so that the only meat the bird can see is on your glove. She may step up well or she may try to feed from your gloved hand while still holding onto the lure. Each time she tries to pull at the meat, lift your hand to the bird's chest height. Eventually the bird will get frustrated and lift one foot to hold down the meat on your hand, once she does this gently lift the gloved hand and the bird should then let go of the lure and place the other foot on your hand. If it doesn't work, and the bird steps off backwards and tries to get the lure again, persevere and start again with the hand over the lure. You and the bird will get the idea and, as long as you are patient, you will end up with a bird that sits nicely feeding on the lure and doesn't even think of carrying.

If the new falcon has not eaten too much during all this time, pop her back on the post and try her to lure again a couple of feet further away; don't forget to whistle as you drop the lure to the ground. If, by now, she has a huge crop call it a day, pick up the falcon and go into safety position, put the leash back through the swivel, take off the creance and put the jesses and leash into the correct carrying position. Wind up the creance, which you should have been practising with for weeks before you got your bird, hood the falcon and go home. You are now getting pretty close to flying free.

There is the occasional falcon that does not respond in the normal way. Every now and again I have to out-think a bird to get the desired response. Last year I trained a Lanneret who would not come to the lure for love nor money, every time I swung the lure the damn bird flew to my fist and hung there. In the end I brought down his block, put him on it on the creance in the middle of the flying ground and dropped the lure right in front of him. Finally that worked and I got him coming about 10ft (3m) from his block before trying with the post. Not all birds are the same or will fit in with what you *think* you know. It is

PICKING UP OFF THE LURE
1 Landing on the lure. If you want to fly a hawk at feathered game, you should use a lure like this one

2 This bird has only one foot on the lure, and her stance shows that she is ready to fly off. Don't approach her at this stage

3 Here the falcon is settled, and ready for you to introduce your fist with the pick-up piece

4 Once on the fist take the lure away, and put it into your falconry bag immediately

really important to understand this, to treat each bird as an individual and to keep an open mind.

I really hope that I am not too dogmatic in the way I think. I am fairly unmoving about the standards in which people should keep, train, travel and fly birds, but I am damned if I think I know it all. As long as you always bear in mind that you should never stop learning you will do all right.

Whistling/Shouting

You may see people flying birds who whistle the whole time, there are even falconers who shout the whole time which is horrid, it's very intrusive and, for me, spoils the whole peaceful aspect of falconry and the countryside. If you see people like this you are seeing people who have not thought about what they are doing and are, in fact, laying in trouble for themselves later. You have to understand what the whistle and the shout are for which, let's face it, is not exactly difficult. They are to attract the bird's attention. If you whistle (or shout) during the whole time the bird is flying towards you, turning, flying away and turning again and coming in, after a very short time the whistle means absolutely nothing to the bird, you might just as well be singing a little ditty. If, on the other hand, you whistle to the bird each time you are going to give her the lure, the whistle means something to the bird and she will soon start to respond to the whistle. Any well-trained bird should turn almost as soon as you whistle.

The shout is used by a falconer out hunting to tell the bird that quarry has been flushed. The bird should know instantly that she should be getting a move on when she hears the shout. We use the shout slightly differently in that we use it to tell the falcon that we are going to give it the lure. The whistle means that she will get the lure seven times out of ten so she is never sure, but the shout *always, always* means that you are going to stop that flight just there. Therefore, if you have a problem with a bird being blown downwind, or being chased by gulls or crows or even buzzards, the shout should turn her and bring her home. But it takes only about four shouts without the accompanying lure to make that falcon into a bird that will not turn on the shout because she no longer believes you. People who call constantly to their birds end up with no method to call the bird in or tell her that 'this time they really mean it'.

In the early stages of training always whistle to the bird every time you call her to the lure and once you start to get her to catch the lure in mid-air always shout. We shout the word 'HO', it's easy to shout, it carries a long way and, yes, in the early stages you will feel like a prat but you will soon get over it. It takes about three to four weeks to train the bird to understand the shout and the whistle. Once she has been flying free for about two months you can then afford to make the whistle a call for nearly always having the lure, but not quite. The shout should always be consistently used to call the bird home or to advise the bird that quarry is flushed.

Coming to the Lure

The following day, for those whose bird did not come to the lure, your bird should have lost a little weight and be more interested. I would almost guarantee that she will come to the lure today if you get it right. Get to the flying ground, after having got all your gear ready, picked up, hooded, weighed, charted down the weight, and carried the bird either walking or on the fist in the car. Creance on, leash off and looped through the strap of the bag neatly so that you never lose it. Bird unhooded and on the perch/post, lure ready before you move away (make this a habit because later on you may find that the bird anticipates you and follows you when you walk away, in which case you may need to get the lure out quickly). Have the loops in place in your gloved hand and the lure ready to come fast if you need it (remembering to have the pick-up piece in the opposite side of the bag so you don't pull it out with the lure). Walk away, swing the lure a couple of times and follow the previous instructions. For those of you whose bird came to the lure yesterday, you need to increase the distance but don't go too far and don't panic if the bird suddenly feels the wind under her wings and flies straight over the top of the lure. Just grab the line with your gloved hand and gently bring the bird down to the ground. Walk slowly towards her, swing the lure a couple of times and drop it just in front of the bird so that she can walk or hop onto it. Then do your very patient, careful, pick up. Take the bird back to the post and try her to the lure over a shorter distance.

When training any new falcon only call her to the lure a maximum of four times. Any more than that and the bird will start to fill up with food or become 'fed up' – and be less and less responsive which is precisely what you do *not* want. Three times, extending the distance by about 10ft (3m) a time is fine. Always take plenty of time with the pick up. Always approach from the front of the bird, low and slow and offering the pick-up piece in an obvious manner. Once the bird is coming 100ft (30m) straightaway, which should take you no more than four days after the bird has been introduced to the lure, you only have two things to teach her before you fly her free: catching the lure and turning.

Catching the Lure

Do your normal routine each day. Get everything ready and in your bag, kitted up before picking up the bird. Proceed with a slow, careful pick up, preferably with the bird bating towards you by now, or at least looking forward to you coming through that door. At this stage always go in with the pick-up piece to encourage the bird. By this time the pick-up piece, and the meat on the lure, should be fairly tough if you can manage it. In this way the bird does not get too much to eat. Hood carefully, if the bird is starting to get edgy about the hood it is your fault (or possibly that the hood is not fitting well). Keep an eye on the soft sides of the falcon's beak, if it starts to show any marks your hood may need the beak opening altered. Also check the inside of your hood, if you see damp marks inside where you would expect the eyes to be, you need a better fitting hood. Take a little time to go back to the early stages and spend five to ten minutes hooding and unhooding the bird and you should get over any problems.

You should weigh your bird every day and chart down the weight. You should also be weighing the food and writing down the food type. You should be able to analyse what weight of food, of what type, does what to the bird's weight at this stage of the training.

By this time you should also be able to use your travelling box, as the bird should really be taming down with all the manning you are giving her after training sessions. Always try to open the box in an enclosed space which I know is difficult if you only have a car rather than my Hi-Top van. Put your hand into the slightly opened box with the pick-up piece and then, opening the box the rest of the way once the bird has shown interest in the food, take the jesses with the other hand. If your bird is not at this stage yet, continue to travel the bird hooded on a fist.

Your falcon should be wearing her bell by now, that is if you didn't bell her at the same time as putting on the jesses, which is preferable. The falcon should have a couple of days to get used to the bell before flying loose. You should also start to get used to using telemetry if you are going to use it. We used to put the transmitter on the leg of the falcon but last year, Blewitt, one of my top Lanners, flew straight through a sheep-netting fence. He fractured one wing and tore the ligaments in one leg, the wing healed well, but the leg took much longer. The leg was injured because the telemetry caught on the wire. Had it been on the tail, we might have lost a couple of tail feathers which would have been far less painful for the falcon. Now we put the telemetry onto the plastic tail mount. You should practise doing this now so that the bird becomes used to carrying the extra weight.

You are now ready to teach the falcon to catch the lure in mid-air. I used to be accused of giving my falcons high catches for the sake of drama. What my critics didn't do was ask themselves why? In fact it has nothing whatsoever to do with dramatic presentation. The reasons are much more practical and mundane. There will, undoubtedly, be times when you fly your bird, or have to call her back to the lure, in areas where the ground cover is quite long. If you drop a lure into heather, long grass or bracken the bird will not see it; if, on the other hand, you have taught your bird to catch in mid-air, you can be standing almost anywhere and you will not have a problem. For those people who intend hunting with their bird, you are most likely to be catching feathered quarry and probably in the air. By teaching the falcon to catch the lure in mid-air you are teaching her to use her feet and her air brakes and you will generally stand more of a chance of catching prey. There are some falcons that are much more difficult to teach to catch the lure than others. Sakers and Gyrs are tricky, probably because they take a good deal of their quarry on the ground. I will go into these more difficult birds later.

Do your normal preparations. You should do the first call to the lure on the ground as usual. Some of you may have birds that will be off the post immediately you swing the lure and these are usually easier to teach to catch the lure. Some birds wait until the lure lands on the ground and you will have to be a little more adept with the lure. Getting a catch is all a matter of time, you just have to watch the bird and imagine that you are trying to throw a ball into her feet. It's a bit like playing catch with a child: you have to make the throw and the catch very easy. Have the lure ready in your bag and go the full length of the creance – this will give you more time to get the lure in the right place – swing the lure and if the bird comes straight towards you, throw the lure into the bird's feet, keeping hold of the stick. Don't forget to shout as the bird approaches the lure and do that for evermore when you are calling her in to the ground or a catch at the end of the session.

When you do a catch let go of the loops that are around your gloved hand so the lure can go a fair distance. Don't do a high catch at this stage, just the height the bird is coming towards you. If you get it wrong leave the lure where it lands and the falcon will probably turn immediately and land on the lure on the ground. If you do it right, and the falcon catches the lure, bring her down gently, moving with the line. In either case, let the bird settle and then do your normal slow and low pick up. Try this three times and those of you who have not practised with the lure should have got it right by the third time. Leave it at that and pick up your bird, feed her and go home.

For those of you whose bird only responds when the lure is dropped on the ground, drop it but keep hold of the loops in the other hand. Then, once the bird flies towards you, quickly swing it up and around once and then into the bird's feet. This is much more difficult and requires more timing and practice with the lure. Try it a few times during one of your practice sessions without the bird. You will find that after a few times the bird should start to come to the lure while it is being swung. Don't worry if she doesn't, I have had a few birds that always waited until the lure was put on the ground before starting the demonstration – it is not a problem.

If you are finding that the bird is slow to respond to the lure, either in the air or on the ground, try bringing her weight down a little, perhaps 1/2oz (15g). If the reverse is happening, and you find you can't get away from the falcon, put her weight up a little and see if that helps.

Carry on with plenty of manning, walking, hooding, putting the bird in the travelling box and taking her out again. Work on all the things, apart from the flying, that you consider the bird needs. You should be feeding a very varied diet of quail, day-old chick, rabbit, perhaps rats and mice, and beef with a vitamin supplement. When you want to give the bird chick, put her on her perch and throw her the food, in that way you will not ruin your glove or get covered in chick yolk. Some people take the yolk out of the chicks before feeding – we don't – we consider that the moisture in the chicks is good for the birds and they love the yolks.

Practise catching the lure for one more day so that you and the bird are really confident in it. But, remember, no more than three or four times per day in one training session. I don't think it is a good idea to do more than one training session per day. The bird then works for you but gets no reward for it. We expect to train a young falcon in three to seven days with only one session per day and we rarely have any problems.

Every so often I get a bird that flatly refuses to catch the lure. I had one this year that nearly drove me nuts! In the end I stood 5ft (1.5m) from the post and, holding my arm up high, held the line so the end of the lure dangled in the air at her eye height 5ft (1.5m) away. She took off and grabbed the lure and I immediately let the line slip down so that she was on the ground with the lure. I only had to do this three times and we were away. Prior to that every time I pulled the lure off the ground, once she had taken off, she veered away and I had to bring her down on the creance which was not doing her any good. However, we got there in the end. It was just one of those times when you have to be open minded.

Turning

The last stage before free flying will require the aid of a helper. This stage may have happened on a missed catch but you need to make sure that the bird will turn after missing the lure. Get your assistant to come with you and hold the end of the, by now, fully unwound creance. Walk to the middle of your flying ground so you have no obstructions around you for the length of the creance. Swing the lure, or drop it on the ground and then pull it up into the swing once the bird has taken off, and as the bird comes towards you do a pass, ie pull the lure away from the bird as she tries to catch it. A pass is when you let some of the line through the fingers of your ungloved hand and aim the lure towards the falcon, then pull the line back through your fingers with your gloved hand. It is impossible to explain in writing – it is pretty difficult to teach physically but you will eventually sort out your own style. A very good lure swinger should let both hands touch as the line runs through the fingers and then let the hands come apart as the gloved hand does the accelerating and the bare hand does the steering of the lure. It should look very easy and graceful and preferably have a fairly slow swing. Some people swing their lures very fast which always makes me laugh as it means they have no way of speeding up the swing to time a more awkward pass. Some people have yards of line out which means they are not in control of the line and some people swing the thing like a helicopter blade over their heads which is bloody silly and can hurt the bird.

Immediately the bird has passed you, drop the lure on the ground and the falcon should turn and come in to land. Your assistant is there to go with the falcon if the turn is larger than the length of the creance. He or she should watch where the bird is going to go and be prepared to run with the bird to give her enough room or alternatively to bring her down gently if it doesn't work and the bird doesn't turn. You will find, as long as you choose a still day and not a windy one, that the bird will turn. Never fly a bird at this stage on a strong windy day. If the bird turns straightaway and it is the first or second time that you have called her to you on that day, fly the bird loose.

Flying Free

You will, by now, have a good idea of what the bird's flying weight is at this stage of her life and fitness. You have got a bell on her and telemetry if you are going to use it. You should be feeling fairly confident with the lure. You have chosen a good calm day and you are not flying the bird too close to dark – so go for it. Put the jesses into safety position which should now be an automatic reaction for you. (Incidentally I always use safety position even when I am carrying a bird that is only wearing hunting straps, by tucking those straps between your fingers you just make the bird more securely held.) Take off the creance and wind it up, if the bird gets edgy put the hood on. But *never leave a hooded bird anywhere unless she is securely tied up*. I have seen falconers, who should know better, put a hooded falcon on the ground completely loose. They are crazy, ignorant and are risking their birds' lives. *Never, never do it*. Take your leash off the strap of your bag where it normally lives during training sessions and remove the swivel from the jesses. This should be very easy to do because the jesses should be nice and supple. Use Ko-cho-line at least three times a week to grease the jesses and keep them soft. If you have Aylmeri or False Aylmeri jesses on the bird, you should also have fixed hunting jesses if you have any sense. Wrap the hunting jesses into safety position, remove the mews or slitted jesses and put them back onto the loose swivel. Now thread the loose swivel, with the loose mews jesses attached, onto your leash up to the button, fold the leash in half and in half again as per normal and thread it back through the bag strap. If you make this a permanent habit you will never end the day having flown your bird and discovering that somewhere along the way the swivel or jesses or leash have dropped out of your bag or pocket.

Removing the Hood

You now have a falcon all but ready to go apart from removing the hood. If you are using telemetry, you should make it a habit to have the receiver and aerial in the car whenever you go out with the bird. Your equipment is all put safely away apart from the lure which should still be unwound and ready to roll. Take the hood off and put it somewhere safe. Put the falcon on the post facing into any minor breeze, behave in the usual normal manner. Walk away, having got the lure ready in your hands before moving, swing the lure and call the loose falcon. Do one pass and either drop the lure on the ground as before or, if you are good with a lure or feel confident, try giving the falcon a catch as she comes around for the second time. If you, or the bird, screw up the catch, don't go for a third pass, just drop the lure onto the short grass on the ground and let the falcon grab it. There you go, the falcon is now flying free. You have no idea how good this feels until you have achieved it. It is so rewarding to fly a bird without having to mess around with swivels and creances etc. If the training has gone well with, maybe, one or two days extra here and there, you should have the falcon going loose in ten to eighteen days. Once things are going well, don't keep the bird on a line for months, you gain nothing and quickly start to spoil the bird, get her free and then the hard work really starts.

The following day, as long as the weather is holding good, take your bird to the flying ground and don't even bother with the creance. Weigh her as usual, do all the normal things and then when you get to the flying ground take off all the jesses, swivel, leash etc, but leave the bird with a bell, a radio transmitter, if you have one, and the hunting straps. Walk away with the lure ready, call the bird, do one pass and try the catch. (If you get it wrong again practise with the lure away from the bird.) Drop it on the ground and let the bird take it there. Do a nice slow gentle pick up and then repeat this. By the end of the session of three or four (at most) flights you should have got maybe three passes and a catch from your bird. Watch the falcon very carefully, at this stage she will be very unfit. If you see her getting lower to the ground, obviously labouring in flight, or see her beak opening, then call her in immediately, remembering to shout and whistle.

Sitting Down
Sometimes you can be unlucky and have a falcon that decides she doesn't want to fly and heads for the nearest telegraph pole. That is why it is a good idea to choose as open an area as possible for training, particularly with no telegraph poles too close. It's also why the summer is a good time for training because the leaves are in the trees and that makes it much more difficult for a young falcon to sit in one. However, having said all that and given people plenty of excuses, nine times out of ten, if a falcon sits down it is the fault of the trainer. Our field is not that open, we have one telegraph pole at the bottom of the field but it is rare for us to have falcons that sit down, it happens occasionally, but not often. In twenty-six years I have only had two falcons that have decided they did not want to fly and both flew straight to the telegraph pole on the second day loose which is very rare indeed.

The art of preventing a falcon from sitting down is to bring her on very slowly. Don't try and have her doing forty stoops at three weeks into flying and don't hide the lure for ten minutes and then wonder why the bird sits down. Put it in terms of yourself, have you ever tried to get fit? It's seriously hard work. Have you ever run 2 miles

(4km) and felt awful the next day because you are stiff and tired? Well if you overfly your falcon early on you will make her overtired, I am sure that they can feel stiff and those are the times when a bird sees a suitable resting post and sits down. If, on the other hand, you always watch to see when the bird is tiring, push her a little more each day, but only slowly, eventually you will end up with a bird that will never even think about sitting down. We have falcons here that have never sat down in 10 years, working nine months per year. If you do push too hard you will spoil your bird for good. We consider that for the first year we are getting the bird fit and we fly her for almost a whole year before resting her for the first moult, and then in the second and third year we start to work on style. Although I have little experience of hunting with falcons – most of what I have caught has been unplanned although occasionally quite spectacular – I have a friend who flies falcons in earnest and he also says that a bird starts to come into its own as a hunting bird in its second or third season.

Falcons and Ground Game

If you want to fly a Saker at rabbits then once you have her coming well to the lure – and Sakers can be difficult to get to catch the lure in mid-air, but persevere – you should introduce the bird to the dummy rabbit in the same way that it is done with hawks (see Chapter 9).

Some people will tell you that by flying a falcon to the lure you will lower her pitch. I don't agree and, as I have some of the highest-flying falcons, I think I have proved that statement wrong time and time again. However, unless you use the lure correctly you won't get a bird to go well. We usually start to get a bird gaining height in the fourth or fifth week, although if you are flying a falcon in nice open hilly country then you can start to get height very much more easily and quickly. We usually try it on days when there is a little wind, but not a gale. As the falcon comes towards you, coming into the wind, hide the lure. If the bird throws up (swings up) over your head, throw the lure out below her and let her catch it. Thus you reward the falcon for going up. If you do this every time the bird gains height, she will get the idea that height brings success. If you can take your bird to a hilly area, let her off at the top and then walk down the hill hiding the lure. This you have to do once the bird is confident and will understand that you hide the lure. She will keep an eye on you and the bird should hold her height and play about above you. Don't leave her up too long in the early days but you will soon find out what helps your bird get up a little height.

Now your bird is flying free you should take her out each day and exercise her to get her fit. Do the job slowly and you will have a good bird for years. Fly her too hard or take her out three times a day and you will quickly spoil her. Have patience and you will succeed. Try flying her in other areas to give different experiences: try different passes with the lure; ground passes where you put the lure on the ground and pull it away at the last minute; overhead passes to push the bird up. Hide the lure for a few minutes and let the bird cruise around, all of these keep the bird interested and happy and improve her flying technique. Once you are happy that the bird is getting fit and is confident flying on various grounds, you are now ready to try to hunt should you wish to.

If you are intending to hunt grouse or partridges you will need a good pointing dog and unless you have one of these you are wasting your time. If you are considering this then you should buy a well-trained dog at least four months before you get your bird so that you and the dog are working well together before you attempt to add in the falcon factor. On the other hand, if you are going to train your own dog then get it eighteen months before the falcon and then it will have had time to grow up and you will have had time to concentrate on training the dog before you start on the bird. If you have not trained a pointing dog before, for heaven's sake get help and advice from an expert. A bad dog will ruin your falconry quicker than anything else.

If you are going to fly at Magpies or Rooks then you just have to get out there and try your falcon at flying at them, there is no substitute for practice. Always try to get close to the quarry which is difficult with the crow family as they are very crafty. You should approach with your falcon hooded but ready to go, ie hunting straps only and telemetry if you have it, but have the brace of the hood open so you can remove the hood quickly. Often it is easier to approach crows by vehicle.

From now on you are on your own. If you can find friends who have flown successfully at quarry, with falcons, enlist their help. Flying a falcon is tremendous fun, takes time and patience and, when you get a top quality bird, is very, very exciting.

Once you have finished hunting for the day remember that the falcon always comes first and so make sure that she is fed and comfortable before stopping at a pub to celebrate. The same goes for your dog if you have one. If it has got wet, or cold, dry it and make sure it has a warm, dry bed if you intend leaving it in the car. To leave a dog wet is unkind, irresponsible and, in very cold weather, might kill it. Even in mild weather it can lead to arthritis later on for the dog and this sort of behaviour is totally unacceptable.

CHAPTER EIGHT

EAGLES

Eagles are definitely not birds suitable for the beginner nor can they be considered to be good pets. They are only suitable for hunting and then only in the right areas. Or, in the right situation. Only with the right bird can they be used for demonstrations. If you are starting in the sport of falconry you should not consider having one. There are some people, however, who live in the wilder, more open, areas who do have the time, the space and the experience with other species who can think of taking one on.

I will not sell an eagle to anyone living in the south-east of England. There are too many people living there, there is nowhere you could go with an eagle where you can guarantee that you won't meet someone taking a terrier for a walk, for example. It is not fair on the bird, the local people or the sport of falconry to fly eagles in such places. If you are adamant about flying an eagle and you live in the South East – move! Scotland, northern England, central Wales, open hilly moorland places – these are the places where eagles show themselves to their best advantage and these are the places to move to if you are serious about having an eagle.

Just because eagles are large birds does not mean that they can take huge quarry. A roe deer is too large for even the big eagles, the deer would be slow in being killed, if indeed the eagle could do it without help, and that is just not good

OPPOSITE

Fairweather, a juvenile Bald Eagle bred at the Centre; definitely not a beginner's bird.

Bald Eagles are being bred in captivity in the UK at various places. They are true fish eagles, but would undoubtedly take rabbits and hares. All the fish-eating eagles I have trained have had a tendency to use their wings as weapons, and to strike at your head when they are at the nervous stage in training – it's very painful, believe me! Eagles should have well-built aviaries not only to keep them safe and secure, but also to make sure other creatures are safe from them

enough. Quarry should be of the right size for the bird to catch and kill quickly. Many people who have flown hawks and buzzards will tell of their birds being injured by squirrels who can easily bite through the tendon on a Red-tail's toe. If an inexperienced eagle takes a fox she could well be injured before succeeding in rendering the fox helpless. Please remember that a decent sized Brown Hare can weigh much more than a male Golden Eagle and some have weighed more than a female.

There is no chance of the South East Asian Hawk Eagles being available in the UK for a long time. They used to be here and to my knowledge there are about three left and they are now very old. None are being bred and so you can forget about them. African Hawk Eagles are being worked with, but so far none have been bred and once they are, the first few will probably go straight back for breeding. One man has bred a few Bonelli's, but the numbers of those are very low just now. Goldens are not readily available in the UK, probably only two have been bred so far, although there are just over sixty birds in captivity. Most of these are not producing young.

The choices are Bald Eagles (these are in pretty low numbers), African Fish Eagles, Verreaux Eagles (these latter two only being bred by me at the moment), Tawny Eagles and, if you go to Germany to buy an eagle, probably Goldens and White-tailed Sea Eagles if you are lucky.

Apart from the Tawny Eagles, you are talking of a price of between £3,000 to £6,000 depending on the bird, so you will have to be fairly flush with money to think of taking up an eagle. As you should have a decent, well-sheltered pen for your bird and that is going to set you back another £1,000, then, as you can see, it is an expensive hobby!

The Fish Eagles, that is the Bald Eagle, African Fish Eagle and White-tailed Sea Eagle are a little more temperamental than the land-hunting eagles, but this could just be the luck of the draw with the particular individuals that I have trained.

A male African Tawny Eagle. The commonest eagle flown in the UK over the last decade has been the Tawny Eagle. They are a nice sized bird, and we have now managed to get our parent birds to rear their own young, which makes the young much pleasanter to handle. Like all the eagles they need to be flown in open country. The difference in watching Chalky, our African Tawny, fly lazily from post to post in our flying ground at the Centre, and then soar up to 1000 feet in open hilly country, makes one really appreciate how good they are given the right flying area.

Housing

Eagles need the same facilities as the *buteos* and hawks, but larger. This applies to the aviary, the bath, the weighing room, the weighing machine, the glove, the travelling box, etc etc. Use the same designs as stated in Chapter 3 and check on the wing-span of the bird before you get her, then double the width of the pen by the wing-span and that will give you the *minimum* size.

Food

Eagles (including the Fish-eating Eagles) will eat pretty much anything. It is a good idea to give Bald Eagles etc fish on a regular basis, but it is not vital. They all eat other food in the wild and seem to do very well on mammalian food in captivity. Ospreys, by the way, need a diet exclusively of fish, which shows how different they really are.

Rabbit, quail, day-old chicks, grown-on chickens and rats are all good food, but as usual the diet *must* be varied. We also use beef when flying them. Mice are very expensive, difficult to get and being so small are not worth the bother. Rats will do just as well. Vitamin and mineral supplements should be used (see Appendix).

Finding Your Eagle

There are very few people breeding eagles. We breed some here at the Centre, and there may be birds advertised in *Cage and Aviary Birds*. As you will not be flying an eagle until you have flown other birds, you will, therefore, have got to know other falconers and other centres and then you will be able to ask around for good breeders of eagles. However, as they are not bred in any numbers, you would be wise to put your name down at least a year before you want a bird.

Do not get a hand-reared bird. Sometimes it is unavoidable, in which case go for a male rather than a female. Most of our young eagles here are either parent-reared or foster-parent reared. With most birds of prey, there is not normally a great deal of difference in temperament between the sexes. You get the odd bad tempered one of either sex but that is due to individual characteristics, not gender. With eagles, the females are more aggressive than the males so, if you have to have a hand-reared bird, the chances are a male will be easier to handle.

Collecting Your Bird

The same principles apply to collecting an eagle as to collecting any other bird. Build a decent sized, strong, lightweight wooden box that will fit the bird and your car. Choose a cool time of the day as eagles are often more susceptible to heat than other birds. Make the usual appointment and arrive on time, don't forget to take a glove so if you have problems on the way home you could at least check the bird.

Once the eagle has been caught up by the breeder give her the usual check over: inside of the mouth; feet; wings and tail. You would be stupid to pay this much for a bird and not get her vetted when you get home. Try to make sure that the eagle has been parent-reared, she is well grown and hard down before you have her. We like our birds to stay with the parents for as long as possible, about five months. If this is not possible we try to put them in a moulting aviary to mature a little before training.

When you get home, arrange for the vet to check her out for you and I would advise a blood sample as well. Your vet will have the blood tested for routine haematological and biochemistry functions and should the eagle ever get ill your vet will have a healthy bird's profile against which he/she can compare any subsequent samples. Jess her up and put her either on a nice piece of grass somewhere quiet and away from people and dogs until dusk, or tethered in your safe, secure pen. You can use a bow perch or a block. Once the bird is settled and has stopped throwing herself around you can add a second perch for the bird. We tend to use a large eagle bow perch and then have a good-sized rock nearby.

Eagles, particularly Golden Eagles, seem to be very susceptible to stress, far more so than the buzzard or falcon family. Therefore, leave the bird alone, only going in after dark to leave some of the food she is used to eating near the perch. Don't start to handle the eagle until the bird has learnt to sit on her perch. Now this is where an eagle's training differs from that of any of the other family groups.

Initial Training

We have learnt, over the years, that feeding an eagle on the fist is not a good idea. They take a longer time to grow up than other birds and can get aggressive if they start to see you as the immediate food provider. We now start to handle the bird as soon as she has settled, and give her as much manning as possible. We don't start to train the bird until she is tame and that can take as long as two months of manning before you start work.

Pick the bird up and man and carry for as long as you can manage the weight. As you are not cutting down the food at all at this stage, it is probably less stressful to leave weighing the bird until she is sitting well on the fist and letting you walk about with her quite calmly. Then start to get her used to being weighed. Have someone put the food down by the perch while you have the eagle on the fist so that the bird finds it there on her return to the perch. As she will not be that hungry, at this stage, she should not be difficult with you in the perch area. If she is, then put the food there in the dark so that the bird finds it the next morning.

By the end of six to eight weeks the bird should be bombproof with you, be easy to pick up, be used to dogs, traffic, being inside, being weighed, being put in the travelling box and so on. She will be used to your hand as you will have been playing with her beak and feet all the way through so that she realises that you have no fear of her. Now is the time to start training.

Flying Field

You can take her to the flying field and get her used to being put on the post and being picked up again. Now put on the creance and I should not need to tell you about safety position, weighing daily, etc because you should know all this *before* attempting an eagle. Put on the creance, then walk away from the bird carrying your bag with lots of small pieces of meat in it: rabbit, quail, beef, whatever you like, but not day-old chick. Throw a piece of meat down onto the ground about 6ft (1.8m) from the bird and see if she will fly down to it. If she does, give her several minutes to settle and then walk to the post and, with a large hand gesture, put another piece of meat on the post and see if the eagle will return to the post. If nothing happens either way, then you should go in gently with *no* meat and pick up your bird and go home. Don't give her any food that day and try again the following day. The idea is to get the bird to fly further and further to pieces of meat on the ground, on gate posts, on your flying perch and

The Verreaux Eagle. This young female in juvenile plumage is just out of the aviary and is trying to sit on a perch that is far too small for her enormous feet (she only sat there for the photo, I promise!).

These are definitely birds that should only be trained by very experienced people, and hunted in areas where they are well away from people and small dogs. The Verreaux Eagle, sometimes known as the Black Eagle, is an African bird and, as you can see by the huge feet, is capable of holding quite large quarry. As far as I know I am the only person breeding them in captivity at the moment. They are very attractive as young birds and moult out to complete black with a white V on their backs. In the wild they hunt Rock Hyrax which are the nearest living relation to an elephant, but not quite as large!

I was delighted when we bred from our African Fish Eagles for the first time in 1992. They are very powerful birds, although not as large as the Bald Eagle. They are also very buoyant in flight, gaining height easily. The young one I am training at the moment has killed the creance several times, as well as anything else that moved on the flying ground, such as twigs! I have no doubt he would be a very effective hunting bird, although how you teach fish eagles to catch fish and not vanish up an inaccessible tree beats me

Tawny Eagles. (Above) The head of Flash, an Indian Tawny Eagle. (Right) Chalky, an adult African Tawny Eagle. There is quite a difference between the Indian and African birds. The Indians are a good deal smaller and more varied in colour. The African race, being larger, are more popular, but either race will take anything up to hare size with no problems

generally all over, so that the bird will respond very quickly. Whistle every time you throw meat and after a while the bird will get the idea. Try her from a low branch in a tree and off all sorts of perches so that she is bombproof.

When you have finished the training session you will need to pick up the bird again to go home. This is where the taming was so important because you do not want to call her to the fist to end the session, you want to be able to go up and just take the hunting straps and have the bird step up with no fuss. Don't go in while the bird has food, always give her time to settle after eating a piece of meat.

Dummy Bunny

Introduce the dummy bunny in the same way as with your other birds, but take it from the eagle differently. Let the bird settle and eat the piece of meat on the bunny and give her a few minutes to relax. Hold the line so that it is tight, throw another piece of meat the other side of the bunny and, as you are holding the line tight, the only way the eagle can get the other piece of meat is to let go of the rabbit. Then you quickly pick up the rabbit before the eagle sees you do it. The other way is to go in and place your bag over the rabbit after the eagle has eaten the reward, and again throw food away from you so that the eagle will go to that and let go of the rabbit. It takes a few goes for the bird to work it out, but it is a really good and safe way to do it.

Flying Free

Once your eagle is obedient and coming well to meat over a long distance, coming out of an easily accessible branch, taking the rabbit and giving it up and allowing you to pick her up at the end of the day, it's time to let her loose. To get an eagle to fly well, and to soar, you will have to take her to an area where she can learn to do this. A small field on the less select side of Gloucestershire is not the place to get soaring eagles but if we take ours to a farm we know which has steep hills and updrafts, the eagles love it!

You should always remember that you are flying a large, powerful bird. To an eagle, a terrier just looks like a short-eared rabbit. Fur coats, collars on coats and gloves look like rabbits and so you, as the owner of the bird, must always be vigilant and keep an eye on what is going on around you and *always keep an eye on your bird*. Eagles are very intelligent, they will often test you to see if they can be the boss, most of the time you just have to ignore them and take no notice. It doesn't hurt to hold the beak and give it a little shake if she is trying it on but we have discovered, especially with hand-reared birds, that if you lose your cool and hit one, they just get worse not better. If you are short of time (or short on patience) then you should not consider an eagle. Time and patience are the keys to training an eagle – and a very strong left arm!

144

CHAPTER NINE
HAWKS

It can be a little confusing to a beginner in falconry as to which are the 'hawks'. The term is used in falconry to cover all hunting birds, including falcons, it is also used to mean the true hawks, but some people call Red-tailed Buzzards, Red-tailed Hawks and also Ferruginous Buzzards, hawks. To check on exactly what family a particular bird belongs to, all you have to do is look at the Latin name and if you see the word *Accipiter* you have a true hawk. The true hawks or *accipiters* are the most nervous and temperamental of the birds of prey to train. Even when they are tame they can throw a wobbler!

In England Goshawks and Sparrowhawks are the only readily available hawks. Although there are Black Sparrowhawks, Cooper's Hawks and Gabar Goshawks in the UK, they are not being bred in enough numbers to satisfy the demand. The Sparrowhawk and Goshawk are very different birds (apart from the obvious difference in size). Very few people would want an imprinted Goshawk but many people, myself included, have flown and liked imprinted Sparrowhawks.

Goshawk

The Goshawk is the largest of the true hawks; it is smaller than a Red-tail and about the same size as a Harris Hawk. There is a fair amount of size variation, but usually the further north the bird comes from, the larger it is, and often the paler in colour. However, breeding Goshawks is not easy, and more often than not it has been a case of using birds that will get on, rather than specialising in putting races of birds together. Size is not really that important; just because a bird is large does not mean that it will be particularly good.

At the time of writing Goshawks are a litle more expensive than Harris Hawks and much easier to lose, but, if you want to catch large game and want to fly one of the true hawks, this is the bird to choose, as long as it is parent or foster-parent reared. An imprinted Goshawk screams a good deal, is very nasty, will mantle, fly at you and generally is to be avoided. I wouldn't risk one for breeding either.

Sparrowhawk

An imprinted Sparrowhawk calls but it is a nice noise and pretty quiet, it is also very useful for helping you to spot your bird in a tree. They stop calling after the first year. They can sometimes fly at you but because they are so small it is not a problem and they give you plenty of warning by dropping their head, putting up their hackles and glancing at you below their brows. Imprinting makes them easier to train and, therefore, puts less stress on them which, with a bird as small as a Sparrowhawk, is a good thing.

Unless you are *very* experienced, and can guarantee that you are going to be around the bird most of the time, I would strongly advise against a male Sparrowhawk. Their minute size means that they can easily go underweight if you are late in flying them and they are prone to going underweight while being flown on very cold days. They are a constant worry and just not worth it. The females, by contrast, are a reasonable size. I love flying Sparrowhawks and am trying to get hold of a young pair this year as I would like to be able to breed one for myself. I had more fun with an imprinted female than almost any other bird. Over a very small area we would have lots of flights at all sorts of things. She would fly to anyone and it was such fun to see her come gliding out of a tree to the fist at the end of the day. It wasn't necessary to get into a car and drive to a hunting ground, I didn't have to try and find rabbits or pheasants, we just had a lot of fun, every day, close to home.

Black Sparrowhawk

Black Sparrowhawks are just like giant European Sparrowhawks but they are definitely not Goshawks. They are nice to fly if imprinted but a

parent-reared Black Sparrowhawk in the UK, with our cool climate, is a nightmare. If they are reared in a group they will still breed and they tend to call a little like a Sparrowhawk. They are not that aggressive but they are hard to get hold of. I have not bred any for two years having lost both my breeding pairs. A good friend and I do have a pair each, but haven't been successful yet.

Cooper's Hawks

Cooper's Hawks can be obtained from the USA, they are smaller than Goshawks and Black Sparrowhawks but larger than Sparrowhawks. They are, to me, more Goshawk than Sparrowhawk. The males are excellent on quail in the USA which means that, in this country, you would probably be limited to Starlings although if you persevered they could be excellent on Magpies. The females can take small rabbits but they are not big enough to be as useful as a Goshawk and, although bigger than a Sparrowhawk, the quarry you can take is fairly limited.

Gabar Goshawks

Gabar Goshawks are in very short supply and although a little more heavily boned than a European Sparrowhawk are about the same size and weight.

Where To Find Your Hawk

Some hawks are easier to find than others, but as you will be experienced by the time you consider taking on a hawk, you will be a little more in the

The European Goshawk is the largest of the true hawks and a very exciting bird to train, fly and hunt. They are difficult and time-consuming to breed, as generally the pair must be separated for most of the year, only being together at the right moment for breeding. This makes them fairly difficult to obtain and not cheap birds to buy. They need a great deal of time invested to make them nice birds to work with. As they need to be flown and hunted regularly a large area of good hunting ground is essential. Under no circumstances should they be flown near other falconry birds. A Goshawk is best flown by a single dedicated falconer who has access to good land and likes to hunt on his or her own; in these circumstances the two should make an excellent team

know as to who has birds and where to find what you want. Order well in advance and don't be disappointed if the breeder fails – breeding true hawks is much more difficult than many other species. Put your name down with a couple of breeders and you will be more successful.

Collecting Your Bird

Pretty much the same rules apply to all birds but anyone who doesn't have a decent wooden carrying box by the time they are ready to collect a hawk should be ashamed of themselves. Collecting a young hawk, as long as the weather is cool and the box is dark and safe, should not be a problem. Hawks are temperamental birds and it is wise to tape the tail with brown paper tape as this will guard against broken tail feathers at least in the travelling stage.

If, by any chance, you ever collect a haggard bird (adult), particularly a fat, untrained one, consider asking *an experienced vet* about using a sedative just for the travelling. You want to minimise the stress caused by the journey.

Arrive with your box, as per usual, having phoned first to make an appointment. Check the bird over thoroughly, leave as soon as the bird is in the box and make sure that the box and the car are kept cool during the whole of the journey. Try to time it so that you arrive with enough daylight to get the bird out and settled before it is dark.

Settling In

Get the bird out and jess and bell her. As with all the birds, put her on her perch and leave her alone for the first three or four days until she has sorted herself out and accepted the fact that she is tethered and is returning to the bow perch after bating. Throw in high quality, high protein food every day at this stage and do not pick up the bird until she is feeding on the perch.

Be careful with your hawk's feet. Sparrowhawks and Black Sparrowhawks have quite fine skin and you need a soft and well-padded bow perch. I use ones that are just covered by polystyrene pipe lagging and then soft leather. As long as you keep them dry they last well and are very good for the bird's feet.

Keeping a true hawk loose in an aviary once she is fully trained and tame is more difficult than any of the other species but if you design the pen well you can do it and it is much nicer for the hawk. Build your aviary with the open wire part above head height so that the bird can look down on people as this always makes them feel much more secure. It is best to experiment with the design as each bird is different and tames differently, which always presents different problems. Remember that Netlon windbreak material is really good on the inside of a pen as the birds can hit it without damaging themselves. Some people also use a permanent tail guard on their bird whilst training and often while travelling. They can be hooked onto the tail bell mount.

Early Lessons

Imprinted Sparrowhawks

If you have chosen an imprinted Sparrowhawk then you will have to collect her before she is three weeks old. You will need a box with torn up newspaper and this is the *only* time, apart from collecting baby owls, that I will recommend a cardboard box. The box will soon get pretty messy with a young hawk so make sure you have a good supply. You will need a decent timber one later on. Check the bird and then get her home quickly. Remember a Sparrowhawk can defecate about 2ft (60cm) at this stage so cover up the seats in your car if you care about them!

As you want to keep this bird tame you must keep her with you during daylight hours (another human will do). Food should be available ad lib and if she is not yet standing well then the food will have to be cut or minced into Sparrowhawk-sized bites. A mixture of quail, day-old chicks, rabbit without fur but with small bones and mice will give you a strong healthy bird, but don't forget to give her a vitamin supplement as well.

You can fit the Aylmeri jesses once the young bird is pulling food for herself, learning to sit on your fist, learning to be carried very gently around on the fist, sitting on the weighing machine and so on. You will also find that occasionally she bails out of the fist, or off your furniture learning to fly. Do not tether her yet. You must not tether a bird until she is hard down and all the feathers are out of the blood, otherwise you could cause permanent feather damage. Fit the anklets and the permanent, thin hunting jesses, this should give you enough to hold onto without them getting in the way of the young bird while she is hopping around.

Parent-reared Hawks

Training a hawk that is parent-reared is difficult and requires more thought. If you remember that hawks react, and then think, rather than the other way around, it all starts to make sense. If you spend hours trying to man a wild hawk, all her experiences of you will tend to be bad. If, on the other hand, you only have her on the fist for short periods in the early stages and lengthen them as the bird starts to relax, the experience for the bird will be much more pleasant.

When you first pick up the bird to try feeding her only try for ten minutes and if nothing happens put her back on the perch. Try again the next day and if she feeds put her back immediately she has finished and the experience for that day will have been a nice one. There is no reason why you shouldn't try feeding her in the morning and if that fails try again the same evening and so on.

Further Training

You should travel your trained hawk in the same way as other trained birds of prey, ie in a well-constructed box that has a side-opening door and a carpeted perch inside. Plenty of ventilation holes are needed and always watch that your car or van does not overheat.

Once the bird is starting to come to the fist the art is to hold her attention. Don't take hours walking away each time she comes to the fist. It is essential, at this stage, to keep her attention and that is not easy. Put her back on the post quickly and get away fast. Call her immediately to you – you are working at the same pace as what little brain the hawk has! What you are looking for is an *instant* reaction from the hawk so that she never learns to be disobedient. *Always, always* whistle every time you call the bird: that whistle must be instilled into her brain so that she reacts every time she hears it. If you find that your bird is not responding quickly, then just get a short jump to the fist and finish the training session right there. If you allow disobedience to go unchecked you are, in fact, training the bird to be disobedient.

Some people have problems getting hawks out of trees but if you have done your job properly and have got the bird coming swiftly to the fist from a post, then the tree should not be a problem. It is risky putting a hawk in a tree with a creance on as they are far more likely to get tangled up than other birds. Hawks are naturally agile and don't have the same problems as eagles or buzzards getting into or out of a tree the first few times. But don't let the bird have too much time in the tree early on. Let her fly in and then whistle and attract her attention straightaway. Make sure you are in a position where the bird can get out easily to start with and then call her down almost immediately.

It is very useful to get birds to turn in mid-air. It's pretty easy with a Harris or buzzard if you have done your job properly and taught them to come to the whistle, but with a hawk you need to trick her by giving only your fist as a convenient landing place. Find an area with no obvious perches and cast the bird off the fist, and then almost immediately whistle and call her back to the fist. The bird is, at that point, looking for a perch anyway and should, if you have taught her to respond to the whistle, turn and come back to you. All you have to do is work on that habit and you will instil even more obedience into the bird.

There is nearly always a good reason when a hawk gets stroppy and sits in a tree for hours. If you know your bird well, you should be able to work out why and then work on the problem. It may be that the bird doesn't like people, or tractors, or dogs, or even something that you can't understand. In most of these cases either you have not done enough work to get the bird used to everything that she might meet while out hunting, or you are not reading the bird properly.

The killing instinct in the *accipiters* is so great that often they will go off and kill something when they are well over a sensible flying weight.

Don't rely on the bird being on a kill before you can recover her. If you do you:
1   have not done your training properly and
2   you are nuts! What happens if you don't kill that day? You spend all day chasing after the bloody bird trying to get her down to all and sundry including the terrier! It also turns the flying of a hawk into an ordeal rather than the fun and exhilaration that it should be.

If you are flying a Sparrowhawk telemetry is probably not necessary. Although you can lose the bird, they are not that expensive to buy and are usually well able to survive in the wild. The other species – Goshawks, Black Sparrowhawks and Cooper's Hawks – are far more expensive and, like all the true hawks, fairly easy to lose. If you are considering one of these you would be very silly not to invest in a decent telemetry set before getting your bird. I say before because you should learn how to use the telemetry properly before trying to find a lost bird.

There is an old saying that Goshawks and Sparrowhawks are subject to having fits. Fits are caused by flying the bird on a poor diet leading to a vitamin or mineral deficiency, or flying it in too low a condition. These days there is absolutely no excuse for a bird dying of fits. If you have a hawk that looks under the weather, put her weight up immediately, put her in your nice warm shed and get hold of your vet straightaway.

The true hawks are great fun to fly but you need to have more time, more patience, more experience and to be more alert to their needs than with the other birds of prey. Unless you have all these attributes don't consider having a hawk.

APPENDIX:
VITAMINS AND BIRDS OF PREY

I was convinced that by feeding a good varied diet to my birds I was giving them all the nutrients that they needed. When Melvyn John from Vydex (manufacturers of different vitamin and mineral supplements as well as other dietary aids) came to see us, I told him that this is what I believed. He then gave a good deal of his time to explain what vitamins and trace elements are, how they work and why they are necessary to birds of prey.

Many people think the same way I did, ie that by giving their birds of prey a good varied diet, nothing else was needed. By now you would think that everyone should know that any single food diet is inadequate. Sadly many people are just feeding day-old chick, often because they have just not thought about their birds and what they may need, or they have taken advice from whoever sold them the bird and been given incorrect information. Some people can't be bothered to find a different food supply and others, because day-old chicks are still relatively cheap, won't pay for more expensive food types.

The tendency is to think that the wild birds must have got it right with a varied diet, eating what and when they can. But wild birds of prey can be just as likely to be deficient in their diet as captive birds and perhaps more so than captive birds properly fed.

The dietary requirements of all living creatures are basically the same in so much as to survive and maintain good health, and to reproduce, the creature will need a regular intake of protein, fat, carbohydrate, vitamins and minerals. Birds in captivity can often be deficient in one or more of the amino acids (constituent parts of protein) and similarly one or more of the vitamins and minerals.

There are eight essential amino acids and fourteen non-essential amino acids. The eight are termed essential because they cannot be synthesised (made) within the body so they must be provided in the food. The non-essential are as important, however, as they can be synthesised from the eight. But even if the eight are provided there is still the potential for a deficient state to exist, if the materials that cause the change in the digestive process (the catalysts in metabolism) are themselves deficient in the diet.

All the vitamins and minerals are essential. The catalysts that are most likely to be deficient are the vitamins that are directly involved in the breaking down and conversion of the food into energy and living tissue. These are the B complex vitamins and vitamin C. This is because they cannot be stored in the body for more than approximately twenty-four hours. Although birds can make their own vitamin C, they are often unable to make (synthesise) enough for their metabolic requirements.

This requirement can change in a split second. For example, if any animal or bird is confronted by sudden physiological stress, such as fright or extreme changes in the weather, the demand for the fuels (nutrients) that the body needs for making the anti-stress hormones, and the energy requirements for the hormonal release, soars. It is at the stage of this sudden demand that the weaknesses in the diet show up so dramatically. If the bird's system cannot cope with this demand, as a result of the deficiency state, she can die within a few minutes. Some of us will know of people who have had birds that have done just this, even aviary birds being caught up for an inspection.

Digestive enzymes are essential in the process for breaking down food, these enzymes are made in the body out of amino acids, and for the efficient utilisation of these amino acids sufficient levels of vitamin C must be present. This means if a deficiency state exists, the digestive process doesn't work properly. Therefore the food and the potential energy the bird would get from it is partially or wholly wasted. B-Complex vitamins are known to be directly involved in the digestive process, and therefore are also essential and are rarely, if ever, present in sufficient quantity in the basic foods – which means they have to be added to the diet. All responsible raptor keepers should be looking to dramatically improve not only the birds' diets but also the birds' well-being and performance by adding a vitamin mineral supplement regularly to the food, thereby fulfilling total dietary requirements of micro-nutrients (vitamins and minerals).

Birds of prey can be divided into three main groups according to what use they are put to:

1   Working bird – flying/hunting birds.
2   Aviary birds – breeding, moulting, resting.
3   Young or growing birds.

All these birds have differing needs in terms of feeding and vitamin and mineral requirements. If there is one element, such as one amino acid or one vitamin or mineral, deficient in the diet that is enough in itself to cause a weakness in the animal, thereby rendering it more susceptible to disease.

Vitamins used prophylactically help to prevent disease. By adding these vital components to the diet, the bird becomes less vulnerable to diseases that are known to be caused by dietary deficiency. You may come across these words when talking to vets.

Working birds will need a higher percentage of fat and protein in their diet. They need all the same vitamins and minerals but in different levels and concentrations. The working birds' energy requirements must be provided before work and replaced after work if the bird is to sustain high performance levels and maintain good health.

Passive birds, in aviaries, resting, will do well on a low-fat, low-protein diet, providing only adequate vitamins and minerals are added. However, throughout the breeding or moulting periods their requirements for a higher energy diet and vitamins and minerals increases considerably.

Young and growing birds can benefit enormously from the right amount of added vitamins helping to prevent all sorts of deficiencies that can be caused during the early part of their life. They need high protein, high energy food. Probiotics also help in the first ten days by giving them 'good and helpful' bacteria.

Birds of prey have a much tougher time than many other species of birds because they are having to break down fat and protein into energy rather than break down carbohydrates. This process can be made more efficient by adding

vitamins and minerals to their diet.

Because the bird's system will firstly convert food eaten into energy, a micro-nutrient deficiency state is often not seen. This state of deficiency is called 'latent hypovitaminosis'. If the bird's system did not convert food into energy first she would die very quickly because the normal functions – body temperature, respiration, circulation, for example – would fail without energy. Therefore the working bird may be flying very well, but if a deficiency state exists, then recovery from the work is slower. Put back to work too soon (or before she has had time to recover fully) the bird will not cope as well. This is often seen as the bird having an 'off day' whereas, in fact, the bird cannot perform as well as a result of a dietary deficiency.

The physiological stress the bird is subjected to then makes her very vulnerable to disease. In addition to the micro-nutrient requirements being fulfilled, a carnivorous bird will be dependent on her system converting fat and secondary protein into energy. This is much harder for the system to do than to utilise carbohydrates, for example, because carbohydrates are relatively easy for the system to use as an energy source. Therefore the digestive process and the conversion of fats and proteins into energy is much slower. However, this food conversion and releasing of stored energy demanded by work is dependent on the function of 'key' vitamins in energy metabolism. Therefore the working bird will require a higher degree of fat in the diet than breeding, moulting or growing birds, plus a vitamin supplement. Birds leading the more passive existence of aviary life will do well on a low-protein, low-fat diet with added vitamins. Growing birds will require high levels of amino acids from protein with some fat for energy and a vitamin supplement.

- Too many calories that are not used will be converted into body fat which is not good for the passive bird.
- Insufficient energy for working birds means they will not cope well.
- Insufficient protein for growing birds will make them slow to make good weight gains and grow decent feathers.
- All these groups will not do well if vitamins and minerals are not present at sufficient levels for them to optimise their potential.

I am often asked how much vitamin supplement should be given to birds – can you overdose them? Well, I am told by a producer of a vitamin supplement that to overdose with vitamins you would have to be giving your birds one hundred times the normal metabolic daily requirements for several months before they suffered from an overdose of vitamins, even those that are fat soluble and stored in the body. This would be very costly in vitamins. Most supplements have directions on the containers and I would suggest that if you are concerned you phone the manufacturer, whose name should be printed on the container.

Calcium, on the other hand, can be very dangerous if given to excess, so supplementing should be done with care and under the supervision of a good, experienced vet. Always feed as much whole food as you can (skinning all food for babies for the first two weeks and longer for Merlins), and by all means use calcium, but under direction. Even today, in June 1993, there are people feeding young birds on meat alone with no bones, and wondering what is going wrong. I find this difficult to believe when so much is known about the dietary needs for young birds, however, my vet assures me that he has had at least two cases this year.

Feed a good varied diet of food that is in itself healthy and from a known source. (Don't go round picking up road kills or using stuff that has been shot with a shot gun.) Keep the food in a clean hygenic manner. Add a good vitamin supplement in the quantities suggested by the manufacturer and your vet, and you should have a happy, healthy bird for years to come.

USEFUL ADDRESSES

The National Birds of Prey Centre
Newent
Gloucestershire GL18 1JJ

Tel: 01531-820286
Fax: 01531-821389
e-mail: jpj@nbpc.demon.co.uk
Visit our website at http://www.nbpc.co.uk

Open to visitors 7 days a week
February–November. Breeds birds; runs courses;
film work; falconry experience days; lectures;
falconry demonstrations; videos, books, mail
order service.

Licensing and Registration Authorities

Wildlife Licensing Department
Department of the Environment, Transport and
  the Regions
Tollgate House
Houlton Street
Bristol BS2 9DJ

Tel: 01179-878154

Import/Export Health Certificates etc

Ministry of Agriculture, Fisheries and Food
Import/Export Section
Hook Rise South
Tolworth
Surbiton
Surrey KT6 7NF

Tel: 0181-330 8222

Clubs and Associations

British Falconers Club
Home Farm
Hints, Nr Tamworth
Staffs B78 3DW

Tel: 01543-481737

British Fieldsports Society
59 Kennington Road
London SE1 7PZ

Tel: 0171-928 4742

The Hawk Board
Chairman
Moonraker
Allington
Nr Salisbury
Wilts

Secretary
Woodley
Reading
Berkshire RG5 4PH

Tel: 01734-696501

The Hawk and Owl Trust
51 Eton Wick Road
Windsor
Berkshire SL4 6LX

Tel: 01753-854393

Raptor Breeders Association
2 Old Bell Cottages
Ludford
Ludlow
Shropshire SY8 1PP

Welsh Hawking Club
Maendy Farmhouse
Church Village
South Wales CF38 1SY

Other Falconry Centres

The Hawk Conservancy
Weyhill
Nr Andover
Hants SP11 8DY

Tel: 01264-773850

The Owl Centre
TAG (Taxon Advisory Group)
Chairman for Owls
Muncaster Castle
Ravenglass
Cumbria

Tel: 01229-717393

Falconry Courses

The National Birds of Prey Centre
Newent
Gloucestershire GL18 1JJ

Tel: 01531-820286
Fax: 01531-821389
e-mail: jpj@nbpc.demon.co.uk
Visit our website at http://www.nbpc.co.uk

The British School of Falconry at Gleneagles
The Gleneagles Hotel
Auchterarder
Perthshire PH3 1NF

Tel: 01764-662231 ext 4347

Hawksport
c/o The Parsonage
Llanrothal
Nr Monmouth
Monmouthshire

Tel: 01600-750300

The Scottish Academy of Falconry
Bonchester Bridge
Hawick
Roxburgh TD9 9TB

Tel: 01450-86666

Veterinary Surgeons Specialising in Raptors

These are all specialist vets but not all are known to me personally, so I cannot vouch for all of them.

Neil Forbes (*Specialist in zoo and wildlife*)
Lansdown Veterinary Surgeons
Clockhouse Veterinary Hospital
Wallbridge
Stroud
Gloucestershire GL5 3JD

Tel: 01453-752555
Fax: 01453-756065

Andrew Greenwood, John Lewis and David Taylor (All *specialists in zoo and wildlife*)

All at: International Zoo Veterinary Group
Keighley Business Centre
South Street
Keighley
West Yorkshire BD21 1AG

Tel: 01535-692000
Fax: 01535-690433

Lance Jepson (*Specialist in exotic animals*)
Fenton Veterinary Practice
21 Portfield
Haverfordwest
Pembrokeshire SA61 1BN

Tel: 01437-762806

Martin Lawson (*Specialist in exotic animals*)
12 Fitzilian Avenue
Harold Wood
Romford
Essex RM3 0QS

Tel: 01708-384444
Fax: 01708-344318

Derek Lyon (*Specialist in zoo and wildlife*)
Gatehouse Veterinary Hospital
Lavister Rossett
Wrexham
Clwyd LL12 0DF

Tel: 01244-570364
Fax: 01244-571215

Peter Scott (*Specialist in zoo and wildlife*)
Zoo and Aquatic Veterinary Group
Keanter Stoke Charity Road
Kingsworthy
Winchester
Hampshire SO23 7LS

Tel: 01962-883895
Fax: 01962-881790

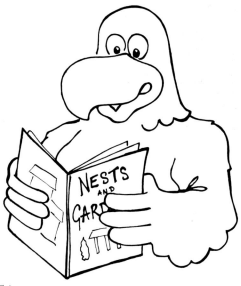

Greg Simpson (*Specialist in avians and exotics*)
Woodlands Veterinary Clinic
Katherine Court
Salisbury Avenue
Warden Hill
Cheltenham
Gloucestershire GL51 5DA

Tel: 01242-255133

Falconry Equipment, Telemetry etc

Martin Jones
Falconry Furniture
The Old Parsonage
Llanrothal
Nr Monmouth
Monmouthshire

Tel: 01600-750300

Vydex Vitamins
Vydex Animal Health Ltd
Cardiff CF5 4AQ

Aviary Equipment

Barns, Timber, Roofing
Fingle Farm Buildings
West Fingle Farm
Drewsteignton
Devon EX6 6NJ

Tel: 01647-21226

Netlon Windbreak Material
Netlon Ltd
Kelly Street
Blackburn BB2 4PJ

Tel: 01254-62431

Onduline Roofing Material
Onduline Building Products Ltd
Eardley House
182–184 Camden Hill Road
Kensington
London W8 7AS

Tel: 0171-727 0533

Wire
Ash & Lacy (Moncasters)
Belvoir Way
Fairfield Industrial Estate
Louth
Lincolnshire LN11 0JG

Tel: 01507-600666

Book and Magazines

Cage & Aviary Birds
King's Reach Tower
Stamford Street
London SE1 9LS

Tel: 0171-261 5000

Falcon Books and Prints
The Parsonage
Llanrothal
Mr Monmouth
Monmouthshire

Tel: 01600-750300

The Falconer's Magazine
D. and L. R. Wilson
20 Bridle Road
Burton Latimer
Kettering
Northamptonshire NN15 5QP

Tel: 01536-722794

St Ann's Books
Rectory House
26 Priory Road
Great Malvern
Worcestershire WR14 3DR

Tel: 01684-562818

I would like to thank IBM for all their help with a word processor and printer, without which I couldn't write books; and my staff, without whose help I would be luggered!

Thanks are also due to John Crookes for providing the line illustrations and cartoons and to John Cross and Steve Chindgren for the photography.

INDEX

Page numbers in *italic* indicate illustrations

INDEX